*L*ove

The Way
To Victory

Kenneth E. Hagin

FAITH LIBRARY PUBLICATIONS

Chapter 1
Characteristics of The God-Kind of Love

And now abideth faith, hope, charity, these three; but THE GREATEST OF THESE IS CHARITY [love].

— 1 Corinthians 13:13

He that loveth not knoweth not God; FOR GOD IS LOVE.

— 1 John 4:8

The Bible says that God is love. It also says that love is even greater than faith or hope. Well, since God is love, then we need to know what love is — that is, the God-kind of love.

In First Corinthians 13:13, the *King James Version* of the Bible translates the word "love" as *charity*. Actually, it is to be regretted that the word "agapē" was translated as *charity* because it doesn't really express the full meaning of the Greek word that is used in this verse.

1

According to the dictionary, the word "charity" means *a benevolent goodwill toward or love of humanity*. But the actual Greek word that is used here is "agapē," which means *the love of God*. Elsewhere in the New Testament, the word "agapē" is translated *love* instead of *charity*.

For example, in First John 4:8, the Bible literally says, "God is agapē." In other words, God is *love*. So the word "agapē" means *the God-kind of love*.

What is agapē or the love of God? Before I answer that, let me show you something interesting about the love of God. The Bible says that love is greater than either hope or faith (1 Cor. 13:13). Why is God's love greater than hope or faith?

Well, first of all, faith won't work without love. In other words, faith is dependent on love in order to work. Galatians 5:6 says, *"For in Jesus Christ neither circumcision availeth any thing, nor uncircumcision; but faith which worketh by love."*

You can readily see that love would have to be greater if faith won't work without it. It takes *love* to make faith work.

And then, second, faith won't work without *hope*. The *New English* translation of Hebrews 11:1 says, "Faith gives substance to our hopes." You have to hope for something *before* your faith can give substance to it. So faith is also dependent on hope.

HEBREWS 11:1
1   Now FAITH is the substance of things HOPED FOR, the evidence of things not seen.

You see, if you don't hope for anything, your faith can't work because it has no goal or object to believe God for. Therefore, faith can't work without hope. Also, faith is dependent on love in order to work. That's why the Bible says that love is greater than either hope or faith (1 Cor. 13:13).

> **1 CORINTHIANS 13:1-3**
> **1   Though I speak with the tongues of men and of angels, and have not charity** [the God-kind of love], **I am become as sounding brass, or a tinkling cymbal.**
> **2   And though I have the gift of prophecy, and understand all mysteries, and all knowledge; and though I have all faith, so that I could remove mountains, and have not charity** [the God-kind of love], **I am nothing.**
> **3   And though I bestow all my goods to feed the poor, and though I give my body to be burned, and have not charity** [the God-kind of love], **it profiteth me nothing.**

The Bible says that even if all the gifts of the Spirit manifested through us, without God's love, it wouldn't profit us anything! It would be as nothing at all. Think about that!

If we understood all mysteries and possessed all knowledge and all faith, but we didn't have God's love operating in us and flowing through us, it wouldn't profit us anything! Even giving to the poor and self-sacrifice are nothing unless we are motivated by love.

Nothing you do will profit you unless it's done from the motive of God's love. You can readily see why the God-kind of love is so important and why the Bible says it's greater than faith and hope.

Also, the Bible says that it's by love — God's love in us — that all men will know that we are His disciples. The Bible didn't say it is by *faith* or *hope* that all men will know we are His disciples. No, it's by God's love demonstrated in and through us that people will know we are Christians.

> **JOHN 13:35**
> **35 By this shall all men know that ye are my disciples, IF YE HAVE LOVE ONE TO ANOTHER.**

How is the world going to know we are Christians? Because we *love* one another!

Love Defined

If the God-kind of love is so important, then we need to know what it is. You understand, of course, that the God-kind of love is not the same as natural human love. Natural human love can turn to hatred overnight, but God's love never fails.

We find God's love defined in First Corinthians chapter 13.

> **1 CORINTHIANS 13:4-8**
> **4 Charity [God's love] SUFFERETH LONG, and is KIND; charity ENVIETH NOT; charity VAUNTETH NOT ITSELF, IS NOT PUFFED UP,**
> **5 DOTH NOT BEHAVE ITSELF UNSEEMLY, SEEKETH NOT HER OWN, is NOT EASILY PROVOKED, THINKETH NO EVIL;**
> **6 REJOICETH NOT IN INIQUITY, but REJOICETH IN THE TRUTH;**

7   BEARETH ALL THINGS, BELIEVETH ALL THINGS, HOPETH ALL THINGS, ENDURETH ALL THINGS.
8   CHARITY NEVER FAILETH: but whether there be prophecies, they shall fail; whether there be tongues, they shall cease; whether there be knowledge, it shall vanish away.

You see, God's love is greater than all these things Paul lists here. It's greater than prophecies, tongues, and greater than knowledge. Why is it greater? Because one day all those things will vanish and pass away. We won't need them anymore. But God's love will never pass away.

There will be no tongue-talking in Heaven, no prophesying, no word of knowledge, or gifts of the Spirit in operation in Heaven. Those things will have passed away. But love — the God-kind of love — endures forever. It won't pass away because God *is* love and He is eternal!

Not only does God's love endure forever, but the Bible says that God's love endures *everything* that may come along. What does it mean to endure everything? *The Amplified Bible* says, "Love bears up under anything and everything that comes. . ." (v. 7). Its hopes are fadeless, and the love of God will never fail.

Now let's read this passage in *The Amplified Bible*, because it defines the God-kind of love more clearly.

1 CORINTHIANS 13:4-8 (*Amplified*)
4   Love endures long and is patient and kind; love never is envious nor boils over with jealousy; is

not boastful or vainglorious, does not display itself
haughtily.
5   It is not conceited — arrogant and inflated
with pride; it is not rude (unmannerly), and does
not act unbecomingly. Love [God's love in us] does
not insist on its own rights or its own way, for it is
not self-seeking; it is not touchy or fretful or
resentful; it takes no account of the evil done to it —
pays no attention to a suffered wrong.
6   It does not rejoice at injustice and unrighteousness, but rejoices when right and truth prevail.
7   Love bears up under anything and everything
that comes, is ever ready to believe the best of
every person, its hopes are fadeless under all circumstances and it endures everything [without
weakening].
8   Love never fails — never fades out or becomes
obsolete or comes to an end. As for prophecy [that
is, the gift of interpreting the divine will and pur-
pose], it will be fulfilled and pass away; as for
tongues, they will be destroyed and cease; as for
knowledge, it will pass away [that is, it will lose its
value and be superseded by truth].

I wish believers would really take time to let this
passage of Scripture soak into their minds and hearts.
Just to walk in the light of these verses would solve so
many of their problems.

For example, notice First Corinthians 13:4 in *The
Amplified Bible*: "Love endures long and is patient and
kind." Now some people endure long, but they're not
patient and kind while they're enduring! They endure
long just because they have to, but they let everyone
know they're enduring too!

For example, sometimes a husband suffers and puts up with things because of his wife, but he's not too kind while he does it. Or sometimes a wife has to suffer and put up with some things about her husband, but she let's him know she's suffering!

However, the God-kind of love endures long and is patient and kind while it endures. And it doesn't weaken, fade out, or come to an end. It never fails.

Closely related to this is verse 7: "Love bears up under anything and everything that comes." You hear some people say, "I just can't love him anymore." Or "I've had it! I just can't love her anymore." Love can. God's love can bear up under everything without weakening or coming to an end.

And since the love of God is in you, then *you* can bear up under everything that comes. Maybe you've said, "I just can't take this any longer." Or "I can't put up with So-and-so any longer." But God's love working in and through you can!

Think about how God is putting up with all of us! I pastored nearly twelve years, and I know that sometimes it can be difficult to put up with some folks. For example, I remember when I was pastoring, sometimes in the nighttime, I'd get to thinking about how God puts up with us, and I'd start laughing about it.

I'd say to the Lord, "Lord, I am wanting to get impatient with some folks, and here You are putting up with all of us!"

Well, God wouldn't ask us to do something we couldn't do. If He told us to love one another, then we can do it. Why? Because God is love, and we're partakers of His love which has been shed abroad in our hearts.

In fact, the most potent characteristic of God is that He *is* love. Love is God's nature. And when we were born again, His love was imparted into our hearts by the Holy Ghost.

The love of God bears up under anything! Don't misunderstand me. I've been there when I wanted to quit from the natural standpoint. But the love of God on the inside wouldn't let me quit because it bears up under everything, and it never weakens, fades out, or comes to an end.

Therefore, if we will just walk in the light of God's love, we will never weaken either. We'll be able to just go on loving folks whether our flesh feels like it or not. We are to love people with the same love that God *is*.

Now look at another characteristic of the God-kind of love. First Corinthians 13:5 says that God's love *"Doth not behave itself unseemly, seeketh not her own. . . ."* Therefore, the love of God operating in and through us "seeketh not her own."

The Amplified Bible says, "Love [God's love in us] does not insist on its own rights or its own way, for it is not self-seeking." That means divine love is not selfish. It doesn't put itself and its own interests first.

Do you seek your own interests first, or do you put the other person's welfare first? Putting other people ahead of your own interests is a good rule to follow to see if you're walking in the God-kind of love.

Too many times believers walk in the natural instead of walking in the Spirit. Have you ever thought about it? Walking in the Spirit is walking in the God-kind of love.

But too many times people walk in the natural and get selfish. And no matter how much it might hurt someone else, they say things like, "I've got my rights! And I'm going to make sure I get them too!"

But the God-kind of love doesn't insist on its own rights. As long as you're going to contend for your rights, you're not going to walk in the love of God.

You'll never be able to believe God fully until you understand and walk in the God-kind of love. Why? Because God *is* love and the God-kind of faith works by love.

So to believe God fully and to operate in the faith of God, you must walk in the love of God.

Love Takes No Account of a Suffered Wrong

One characteristic of the divine kind of love is that it never takes account of a suffered wrong. First Corinthians 13:5 in *The Amplified Bible* says, "Love [God's love in us] . . . takes no account of the evil done to it — pays no attention to a suffered wrong."

Your flesh would rather hear something different, wouldn't it? But this verse contains love's thermometer. Are you touchy, fretful, or resentful? Are you always taking account of the evil done to you?

This is the divine love gauge. It is easy to find out whether or not you're walking in love by looking at your love walk in the light of this verse.

As long as you take account of the evil done to you, you're not walking in love. But as long as you walk in God and in the God-kind of love and stay full of the Holy Spirit, you won't take account of the evil done to you.

As long as you're taking account of the evil done to you, you won't be able to believe the best of every person. Have you ever noticed that natural human love is the opposite of believing the *best* of everyone?

It is always ready to believe the *worst* of every person. In fact, some folks are always looking for something to try to get on someone else so they can accuse them or talk about them.

I traveled for years in the field ministry, and many times preachers would say to me, "Have you heard about So-and-so?" and they'd start to tell me something bad about someone else.

I'd always say to them, "I refuse to believe anything bad about anyone. I believe the best of everyone." And more often than not it turned out to be just a rumor that was going around.

God's love is ever ready to believe the best about every person. Since God is love, that means God is ever ready to believe the best about each one of us!

After I was born again, something on the inside of me in my spirit seemed to compel me to believe the best of everyone. My flesh didn't necessarily want to. But the Bible says that the love of Christ in our heart compels us to do what is right (2 Cor. 5:14).

That's why we should let the love of God compel us to think the best of everyone so we won't be touchy, fretful, or resentful. Then it will be much easier to take no account of the evil done to us.

First Corinthians 13:8 says that God's love never fails, fades out, becomes obsolete, or comes to an end. Since God is love, then if *love* could come to an end, *God* could also come to an end. But God never fails, and neither does His love!

Some people think it's a point of weakness to take no account of evil done to you and to pay no attention to a suffered wrong. But it isn't. It's the God-kind of love in action. And the closer you walk with God and the more His love dominates you, the more you'll forgive and pay no attention to suffered wrongs.

Over the years, when someone did something wrong to me, I've had people say to me, "I wouldn't take that if I were you!"

I've even had people tell me that it was a weakness in my character because I wouldn't fight people who fought against me. They said it was a character defect that I never paid any attention to a suffered wrong. They'd make comments like, "He sure told you, didn't he?"

I'd answer, "No, no. He didn't tell me off. I never paid any attention to what he said in the first place." I haven't paid any attention to a suffered wrong in all these years. I just keep on preaching and loving and staying healthy.

Fellow ministers have even told me, "Boy, I sure wouldn't take that if I were you. I wouldn't put up with that. If I were you, I'd do something about it!" But I didn't do anything about it. I just walked on in love and stayed healthy. I've noticed that some of those who said that to me died prematurely.

I just learned that when people say something against me or do me wrong, it will hinder my walk with God if I criticize them or retaliate by saying anything bad about them.

Besides, I know that the Bible says love never fails, so it's better to do something good for people who wrong me so I can put God's love to work in the situation.

Many have failed and even died prematurely because they lived so much in the natural that they were always fussing and fighting. And that has an effect upon people, not only spiritually, but it has an effect upon them physically.

I remember I went to pastor a particular church where the former pastor had experienced quite a bit of difficulty when he pastored that church. When he finally left the church, half the people were for him and half of them were against him.

He stayed in that town, and he would visit his former church members and collect their tithes and offerings, even though he wasn't pastoring that church anymore. And he would tell my church members that they were out of God's will because *he* was still supposed to be the pastor.

Finally, the officials of that denomination found out about it, and they came to me because I was the new pastor. They said, "Brother Hagin, all you have to do is say the word, and we will dismiss him from the fellowship and take his ministerial papers away from him."

I said, "No, I'm not going to do it. If he keeps going like he is, he won't make it spiritually anyway. But I'm not going to contribute to his downfall."

You see, love takes no account of a suffered wrong. But once I get involved in contributing to someone else's downfall, it will affect me spiritually and physically. I don't want anything to hinder my spiritual growth.

And I don't want to give the devil an open door to put sickness or disease on me either. I don't like sickness. I was sick for the first seventeen years of my life, and I don't want any part of sickness. And I know that in order to walk in health and to grow spiritually, a person has to walk in love toward others.

I'd just rather let the Lord attend to any wrong done against me, rather than getting involved myself. Because once I get involved, I will probably get into trouble spiritually. Besides, two wrongs never make a right.

So I said to those officials, "No, I'm not going to say anything against him. Instead of contributing to his downfall, I'm going to help him. I'm going to contribute to his success by praying for him."

Then in the process of time, I had the opportunity to be a blessing to this man. He was a carpenter and built a house for his family. I went to him and said, "I'll wallpaper your house for you."

When I finished wallpapering his house, he asked me, "How much do I owe you?"

I replied, "You don't owe me a thing. The Lord told me to do it for you as a love offering."

When I said that, he and his wife began to cry. They admitted that they had visited my church members, and they repented. They said, "But, Brother Hagin, we never spoke against you to any of your church members."

I said, "Well, in the first place, you didn't have anything you could say against me. But, on the other hand, dear Brother and Sister, did you ever stop to think about it?

"When you visited some of my church members and said that they were out of God's will because you should still be the pastor, you were creating strife and division. You were really speaking against me, because I'm the pastor of that church now. God put me there. So you might as well have been speaking against me."

They both said, "We were wrong. Will you forgive us?"

I said, "Sure I will." Then I invited them to come back to the church and preach. It was important that this former pastor be restored to the people and get things right with that congregation so he could go on in the ministry.

But they didn't want to come back to the church to preach. They said, "No, we can't come back and preach. The people don't like us."

I had never allowed the people in my congregation to talk against this couple. That not only violates the law of love, it is dangerous. I don't want to talk against any of God's servants.

Divine Love Is a Peacemaker

Remember in the Old Testament when Saul was backslidden and trying to kill David, David wouldn't harm Saul even though he had many opportunities to kill him. David said, "*Touch not mine anointed, and do my prophets no harm*" (1 Chron. 16:22; Ps. 105:15).

I don't want to be guilty of touching God's anointed in any way. So I tried my best to build goodwill toward this former pastor in the people's eyes because God's love in us is a peacemaker.

Divine love is a peacemaker. And divine love will always win out in the end. So I persisted in asking this couple to come and preach at my church, and finally they agreed.

When this former pastor got up to preach, he said, "Folks, I want all of you to forgive me. I've been wrong. I said that God couldn't bless this church because I thought I was still supposed to be the pastor. But I see that God is blessing this church, and I want everyone to know that I'm thrilled about what God is doing here." When he repented for his wrongdoing, the people forgave him.

Love never fails! Love always wins! Divine love is a peacemaker. The Bible says, *"And above all things have fervent charity among yourselves: for charity shall cover the multitude of sins"* (1 Peter 4:8). It was so much better to reunite this former pastor and his wife with that congregation than to allow strife and discord to prevail.

When this couple lost that church, they had been thinking about leaving the ministry altogether. But because they repented and were reconciled to the congregation, instead of quitting the ministry, they went on to build a church in another place, and God blessed them.

That was so much better than allowing strife to ruin this couple's ministry! That's why I'm not going to contribute to anyone's downfall. Love takes no account of a suffered wrong!

I'm just going to keep on praising and worshipping the Lord no matter what people do to me or say about me. And because I'm endeavoring to walk in the divine law of love, I'm going to keep on enjoying good health and the blessings of God too!

Let folks say and do what they want to, but I'm going to endeavor to walk in the God-kind of love! Love is the best way. And it is *our* way because the God-kind of love has been shed abroad in our hearts.

Learn To Let God's Love Dominate

Just walking in the love of God would solve all of our problems at home. And it would solve all of our problems in the church too. In fact, it would solve all of our problems in our marriages.

That's why the Bible tells us that we are to make the love of God our great aim in life. *The Amplified Bible* says it this way: "Eagerly pursue and seek to acquire [this] love — make it your aim, your great quest. . ." (1 Cor. 14:1).

Since God's love is so powerful and enduring because it never fails, why don't more believers do what the Bible says and make the love of God their aim and their great quest in life? In fact, how many of us can honestly say we have made God's love our great quest in life?

Yet God's love working through us and reaching out to others can change anyone, even the most vile criminal, because the love of God can soften the hardest heart. The love of God can transform anyone.

The God-kind of love can even transform a marriage. I make mention sometimes about a minister's wife who called my wife for help because she was just about to leave her husband. Her husband was both mentally and physically abusive to her.

I told my wife, "See if you can get both of them to come over so we can talk to them."

When they arrived, among other things I asked them if they had *The Amplified Bible*. They did, so I told them, "On a 3 x 5 card, write out First Corinthians 13:4-8. Then when you go to bed at night, both of you read those verses out loud. Then read them again when you wake up in the morning."

After several weeks, the wife called my wife back and said, "You know, every morning and every evening we've done just what Brother Hagin said to do. We've read those verses on the love of God out loud."

Then she said, "Every single day since we've been reading those Scriptures, my husband has apologized to me. He's said, 'I can't believe I mistreated you as I did. I can't believe I said those things to you.'"

And instead of allowing his flesh to dominate him, this man began letting his spirit dominate him. The love of God had already been shed abroad in his heart or his innermost being. He just had to learn how to tap into that love.

When he started letting the God-kind of love dominate him, his wife told us, "He's just become a different person! Not only has *he* become a different person, but so have I.

"I realized that to a large extent, I'm to blame for him finally blowing his top because I just kept nagging him. I should have kept my mouth shut. But we're both different people now because the love of God has changed us." God's love never fails!

This was several years ago. My wife and I have seen this couple in more recent years, and they're very happy together.

They told us that their ministry is prospering and their lives are better — just because they learned how to let the love of God dominate them. The God-kind of love changed them both.

Thank God they learned where the answer is. The answer to so many problems in life is found in this statement: *God's love never fails*!

Therefore, if *you* learn to walk in love, then you're never going to fail either, are you? I'm talking about divine love — God's love in us — not human love.

And if a husband and wife will walk in God's love, their marriage won't fail either. It would be absolutely impossible! You see, God's love is in us, but it is up to us to put it into action and exercise it so it can grow and develop.

Since God's love will not fail, we need to find out more about this kind of love. We need to find out how to develop God's love and how we can cause it to grow and mature.

Love Is a Fruit of the Spirit

You need to understand that love can grow and develop because it is a fruit of the spirit, and fruit grows. When the Bible talks about the fruit of the spirit, it is not referring to the fruit of the baptism of the Holy Spirit.

Love is the fruit of the recreated human spirit. You receive the fruit of the spirit when you are born again. In fact, love is the first fruit of the spirit that the Bible mentions.

GALATIANS 5:22,23
22 But the fruit of the Spirit is LOVE, joy, peace, longsuffering, gentleness, goodness, faith,

23 Meekness, temperance: AGAINST SUCH THERE IS NO LAW.

Moffatt's translation says, "But the harvest of the Spirit is love, joy, peace, good temper, kindliness, generosity, fidelity, gentleness, self-control: — there is no law against those who practice such things."

The Amplified Bible says, ". . . Against such things there is no law [that can bring a charge]" (v. 23). If you're walking in love, no charge can be brought against you!

In Galatians 5:22, the translators of the *King James Version* capitalized the letter "s" in the word "spirit," leading us to believe it refers to the Holy Spirit.

But *W.E. Vine's Expository Dictionary of New Testament Words* points out that there is only one Greek word for "spirit" and that is "pneuma," which means *breath* or *spirit.*

Therefore, sometimes it is difficult to tell whether the Bible is talking about the Holy Spirit or the human spirit, unless it specifically says the *Holy Spirit* because the same Greek word, "pneuma," is used for both words.

It is obvious that the Bible is talking about the human spirit here in Galatians 5:22, not the Holy Spirit. How do I know that?

Well, ask yourself the question, *Where does fruit grow?* Fruit grows on the branches because of the life that comes from the trunk or the vine of the tree. Jesus said, *"I am the VINE* [trunk]*, ye are the BRANCHES: He that abideth in me, and I in him, the same bringeth*

forth much fruit: for without me ye can do nothing"
(John 15:5).

Who are the branches? The Holy Spirit? No, *we* are
the branches. Fruit grows on the branches, not on the
trunk of the tree. Therefore, since we are the branches,
we know that the fruit of the spirit refers to the fruit of
our recreated human spirit.

The fruit of love is produced from our born-again
human spirit because of the life that comes from abiding in the Vine, the Lord Jesus Christ.

Jesus used the illustration of a tree to teach us
about the fruit of the recreated human spirit.

In John 15:4, Jesus made an amazing statement. He
said, *"The branch cannot bear fruit of itself, except it
abides in the vine."* Love is the first fruit of the born-
again human spirit because of the life that comes from
abiding in the life of Christ within.

We used to have a pear tree in the backyard of our
little frame home in Garland, Texas. It was a sugar
pear tree, and those pears made great preserves. When
I'd go out there and pick pears off that tree so my wife
could make preserves, I never did see those pears growing anywhere else except on the branches.

Now why did that fruit grow out there on the
branch? Because it was receiving something from the
trunk or the *vine* of that tree. The life that was in that
vine flowed out into the branches.

Therefore, we can see that the fruit of the spirit is
the fruit of the recreated human spirit because of the
life of Christ within our spirits.

That life has been imparted unto our spirits through the Word of God by the Holy Spirit. So the God-kind of love is written in our hearts or spirits.

If we'll just let that love dominate us, what a difference it will make in our lives! You see, because love is a fruit of the recreated human spirit, it can grow and be developed. Because the love of God has been shed abroad in our hearts, it's up to us to do something with that love nature.

In fact, even though the love of God is in us because it's been shed abroad in our hearts, it won't really work or be developed unless we put it into action. You see, developing and exercising the God-kind of love is up to *us*.

We can feed the love of God in our hearts on God's Word, exercise it, and it will grow because love is a fruit! That's why we can develop in love because fruit can grow and develop.

In fact, think about it. Fruit isn't produced fully mature; it doesn't suddenly appear on the branches fully grown and mature. It starts out as a little bud, and it has to mature by taking its life from the vine — from the trunk of the tree.

Let me illustrate how the fruit of love can grow, develop, and be increased. I've been married for more than fifty years. When I married my wife more than fifty years ago, I thought I just couldn't love her any more than I did then. But now, fifty some-odd years later, it seems as though I hardly loved her at all back then because I love her so much more now.

When my wife and I were first married, we promised each other that we'd always be sweethearts. And do you know that we still are today! For example, we've made it a practice over all these years of marriage that at every meal after we've prayed, we always kiss each other. We practice an attitude of love.

Love practiced brings great rewards. Love always puts the other person first. Now I'm not perfect, but I have always endeavored to put my wife first. Through all of these years, I've tried to do what pleases her.

For example, when I'm home, I always cook breakfast. I've done that throughout our more than fifty years of marriage. And when I make breakfast, I always give my wife the best egg, the best piece of bacon, and the best piece of toast because that's what love would do.

Natural love? No! The flesh would say, "I want the best piece of bacon! I want the best of everything! I want my rights and my own way!"

But I refuse to let my flesh dominate me. That would be wrong thinking, and I won't allow wrong thinking to dominate me. I let the love of God on the inside dominate me.

Well, since the love of God has been shed abroad in our heart, then we've got to let our heart dominate us, not our head — not our natural thinking.

But, you see, the less you talk about your love for one another and communicate it to one another, the further apart you grow. You could eventually grow so far apart that you could find yourself wondering why you married that person in the first place.

That's absolutely the truth! The same thing is true spiritually. The less you talk about God and the less you read the Bible or confess that you love God, the more your fellowship with God sort of wanes and grows sour. After a while, it's almost like you don't know whether you're saved or not!

But the more you confess how much you love God and His Word, the more your love for Him will grow and develop. And Jesus will become more real to you.

So constantly feed the love nature that is in your spirit by exercising the divine kind of love. If you constantly exercise it, it will grow and develop.

The fruit of love grows, develops, and increases! The love of God increases by confessing it and by acting on your love. Love is revealed by word and action. Act in line with the God-kind of love and watch your love grow and increase.

Thank God, we can grow in love, because fruit grows. But think about this. The love of God won't really work for us unless we put it into action. Love won't grow and be developed unless we exercise it. So it's up to each one of us to see to it that our love is developed by exercising it.

The Bible said, "Perfect love casts out fear" (1 John 4:18). Now I don't know whether any of us has ever gotten to the place where we are perfect in love yet, but thank God, we *can* grow and develop in love! Thank God, we can be perfected or matured in love.

That doesn't mean we are going to be perfect now in this life. And it doesn't mean we are going to be perfect as God is perfect. But it means that we can mature in the God-kind of love. And the fruit of love ought to at least be beginning to bud in our lives!

It may take time for the fruit of love to mature. We may not see the full-grown mature fruit yet, but at least we can see some buds starting to appear, and we can know our love is growing and developing.

I was holding a meeting one time, and three pastors came to visit my services. After the meeting, we all went out to eat and fellowship together. These pastors began talking about the subject of the love of God.

I was just listening to their conversation. I wasn't talking much. You know, sometimes you can learn more by listening than you can by talking because you already know everything *you* know!

Anyway, these pastors got to talking about how much believers fail in the love walk. And one of the pastors spoke up and said, "I'll tell you what! We need to pray! We need to pray that God would give us love. We just don't have the love of God as we ought to have."

I didn't say anything. But I thought to myself, "Since the love of God has been shed abroad in our hearts, then if a person doesn't seem to have love, he's just got to learn to walk in the light of what he already has. That's where the problem is."

Finally, one of the pastors asked me, "Brother Hagin, what do you think about it?"

I asked, "Do you really want to know?"

"Yes!" he said.

"Well, if you fellows don't have any love, as you just got through saying, then you need to get saved!" They looked at me in astonishment — sort of like I'd slapped them with a wet dish rag.

I continued, "The way you talk, we don't have the love of God. But the Bible says, 'We know we have passed from death unto life because we love the brethren.' And if we're saved, we've got the love of God in our hearts because the Bible says the love of God has been shed abroad in our hearts by the Holy Ghost" (1 John 3:14; Rom. 5:5).

The pastor who had asked me this question looked sort of startled, and then said, "You know, you're right!"

He said, "I tell you, what we need to do is just pray that God would give us a baptism of love. Let's just pray that He would baptize us in His love!"

I said, "There is no such thing as the baptism of love. Love is not a baptism. Love is a fruit of the recreated human spirit by the work of the Holy Spirit in the new birth.

"It's not a matter of needing to pray that God would send us love, because He's already given every believer a measure of the God-kind of *love*, just like He's already given every believer a measure of the God-kind of *faith*. It's just a matter of stirring up and using what's already on the inside!"

I said, "If you're saved, you already have a measure of the God-kind of love. You can pray until you are blue in the face that God would give you more love, but the love you have will never be increased until you feed it on God's Word and exercise it so it can develop.

"If you develop it, then it will be increased. Feeding it on the Word and exercising it is the way you increase the God-kind of love. Love has to be exercised before it will produce results because love is a fruit of the spirit. But if you will be faithful to exercise the God-kind of love, it will produce great fruit."

The God-kind of love is a fruit. The Word says that if we abide in the Vine, we will bear much fruit (John 15:1-8). So if a believer doesn't have any love, evidently he's not abiding in the Vine and drawing his nourishment from the Vine as he should be.

What happens a lot of times is that believers get taken up with natural things, and that's where they dwell. Therefore, they don't take advantage of what already belongs to them as they should. They don't take time to be nourished by the Vine by communing with the Lord Jesus Christ and His Word. That's why we need to put spiritual things first.

All you need to do to grow in love is abide in Him and let Him abide in you through prayer and the Word and communion with Him. Then exercise the love that you have on the inside.

Don't get discouraged if all you can see are just a few buds of the fruit of love on the branch. Just keep on abiding in Him.

Spend time waiting upon Him and feeding on His Word, and then that love that is budding will blossom and finally bring forth much abundant fruit to God's glory.

Walking in the Spirit Is Walking in Love

I want to point out something else to you about walking in the love of God. In the Book of Galatians, Paul talks about walking in the Spirit. Remember this letter wasn't written just to one church. This letter was written to be read throughout the churches in Galatia.

> **GALATIANS 5:16**
> **16 This I say then, WALK IN THE SPIRIT, and ye shall not fulfil the lust of the flesh.**

A lot of times when believers talk about walking in the Spirit, they sort of get misty-eyed and foggy-headed. They seem to think that walking in the Spirit is some kind of mystical experience where they just sort of float around caught up in the Holy Spirit.

But really walking in the Spirit is very simple. Walking in the Spirit is walking in the *fruit of the spirit*. Walking in the Spirit is walking in *love*.

Notice what Paul says about walking in the Spirit. First he lists the works of the flesh. Then he lists the fruit of the spirit.

> **GALATIANS 5:16,18-25**
> **16 This I say then, WALK IN THE SPIRIT, and ye shall not fulfil the lust of the flesh. . . .**
> **18 But IF YE BE LED OF THE SPIRIT, YE ARE NOT UNDER THE LAW.**

**19 Now THE WORKS OF THE FLESH ARE MANI-
FEST, which are these; Adultery, fornication,
uncleanness, lasciviousness,
20 Idolatry, witchcraft, hatred, variance, emulations, wrath, strife, seditions, heresies,
21 Envyings, murders, drunkenness, revellings,
and such like: of the which I tell you before, as I
have also told you in time past, that they which do
such things shall not inherit the kingdom of God.
22 But THE FRUIT OF THE SPIRIT is love, joy,
peace, longsuffering, gentleness, goodness, faith,
23 Meekness, temperance: AGAINST SUCH
THERE IS NO LAW.
24 And they that are Christ's have crucified the
flesh with the affections and lusts.
25 If we live in the Spirit, LET US ALSO WALK IN
THE SPIRIT.**

Paul said, "Now the works of the flesh are manifest. . ." (v. 19). Or we could say it this way: "If you walk
in the flesh, then the works of the flesh will be manifested, and they will dominate you."

Then Paul goes on to list the works of the flesh:
adultery, fornication, uncleanness, lasciviousness, idolatry, witchcraft, hatred, variance, emulations, wrath,
strife, seditions, heresies, envyings, murders, drunkenness, and revellings.

But in verse 22, Paul also lists the fruit of the spirit:
love, joy, peace, longsuffering, gentleness, goodness,
faith, meekness, and temperance.

Notice what Paul says about walking in the Spirit:
*"This I say then, Walk in the Spirit, and ye shall not
fulfil the lust of the flesh"* (Gal. 5:16).

Well, how do you walk in the Spirit? To walk in the Spirit is to walk in the fruit of the spirit. To walk in the Spirit is to walk in love! In other words, walking in the Spirit is walking in love, joy, peace, longsuffering, gentleness, goodness, faith, meekness, and temperance.

Then Paul says, ". . . *against such there is no law.*" In other words, when you are walking in the fruit of the spirit, there is no law that can bear witness against you because you will be fulfilling all the requirements of the Law.

So putting it simply, we can say that to walk in the Spirit is to walk in the nine fruit of the recreated human spirit. That is the essence of what walking in the Spirit is all about.

Love Worketh No Ill to His Neighbor

Now look at Romans 13:10 because there is a truth we need to see about the God-kind of love in this verse.

ROMANS 13:10
10 LOVE WORKETH NO ILL TO HIS NEIGH-BOUR: therefore love is the fulfilling of the law.

Another characteristic of the God-kind of love is that *"Love worketh no ill to his neighbour"* (Rom. 13:10). Well, you could read it this way and do that verse no injustice: "Love works no ill to anyone."

Over the years, my wife and I have had many opportunities in the ministry to exercise the God-kind of love so our love would grow and develop.

For example, one time we went to preach for some folks, and we had just enough money to buy gasoline to get to their church. We arrived at the church in time to preach that evening, and after the service we were hungry because we'd been traveling all day with very little to eat.

We were staying with the pastor and his wife in their parsonage, so we thought surely they would give us something to eat when we came home after the service.

But they didn't take us out to eat after church or give us anything to eat at their house. They just went to bed, so we went to bed hungry. The next morning we got up hungry, but they had already gone.

My wife said, "Maybe they went out to get something to fix for breakfast." But they didn't come back. Later she said, "They'll probably come back at lunch and take us out to eat."

Well, they didn't come back for lunch either. We didn't have a cent in our pockets because we'd used every bit of our money just to get to that town to preach.

Finally, they came in about church time and got ready to go to church. But they never said anything about dinner or about feeding us. They didn't even ask us if we'd had anything to eat or if we were hungry.

It had been a day and a half since we'd eaten anything, and we were hungry. It's one thing when you're fasting and seeking God. Then you expect to deny the flesh! But we weren't fasting. We were just going hungry because there wasn't anything to eat.

Then after we finished the church service the second night, we thought they'd probably offer us something to eat, but they never said a word about it. They went to bed, so we went to bed too.

We got up the next morning, and they had already left. We thought they would probably come back by noon and take us out to eat or at least give us some food. But they didn't come home.

Finally, we went into the kitchen to see if we could find something to eat because by then we were really hungry. We found one shriveled hot dog, one egg, and one stale piece of bread. We fixed the toast, boiled the hot dog, cooked the egg, and we each had a half a piece of toast, a half a hot dog, a half an egg, and a glass of water apiece.

I said to my wife, "I know what I'm going to do!" You see, your flesh and your mind can get stirred up when people do you wrong. That's why the Bible says you've got to keep them under subjection to your spirit.

I said, "I'm going to call the district superintendent, and ask him, 'What kind of ministers do you have in this district, anyway? We haven't had anything to eat for two days!'" You know, if you're not careful, in a situation like that, your flesh will want to take over.

So I went to the phone and started to call the district supervisor, but something on the inside constrained me. It was the love of Christ constraining me.

I came back and said to my wife, "I can't do it. I didn't call the district supervisor. Bless their hearts! People who act like these pastors are not going to make it spiritually anyway, but I'm not going to contribute to their downfall. I'm not going to be the one to trip them up.

"I don't care if they did do wrong, I've got to walk in love whether they do or not because the Bible says that love worketh no ill to his neighbor."

Well, that couple finally came in before church on the third day and never said anything about dinner or even asked us if we were hungry. We went to church, and afterwards they just brought us home and didn't offer to feed us anything. They hadn't even given us an offering so we could buy something to eat.

By then, it felt like my stomach was rubbing my back bone! When you go without food for several days, your flesh gets to crying out! I said to my wife again, "I'm going to call the district superintendent and ask him what kind of pastors he has in this district!" If you go to paying attention to your head and your flesh, you'll get into trouble.

I went to the telephone to call him, but again, something on the inside of me wouldn't let me do it. The love of Christ constrained me.

I said to my wife, "No, I can't do it. I've got a mind to get in the car tonight when the service is over and just leave. But I couldn't do that either.

In the first place, people in the congregation would ask the pastor, 'Where is Brother Hagin?' Then they would wonder why I left, and it would look bad for the pastor."

But by the next day, we were hungry! I started to call the district superintendent again, but I just couldn't do it.

Instead, I said to my wife, "I can't do it. These dear ones, bless their darling hearts, are never going to make it in the ministry acting this way. But I don't want to contribute to their downfall. I'll stay through Sunday. I'm going to do right whether these pastors do or not."

People who don't have any more character or concern for others than that are never going to make it anywhere, much less in the ministry.

In fact, this couple never should have been in the ministry to begin with. But I'm not going to contribute to their downfall, because then it would hurt me spiritually. Sooner or later this pastor is going to reap whatever he sowed, but I'm not going to help him reap it.

Besides, love worketh no ill to its neighbor. Love takes no account of a suffered wrong. Love — God's love — is longsuffering, patient, and kind.

Finally, one of the church deacons came to visit us, and he began questioning me. I saw that he knew something wasn't right. But I didn't want to hurt the pastor by confiding in one of his own deacons. Love worketh no ill to his neighbor. So I did my best not to say anything that would hurt the pastor.

The deacon finally said to my wife and me, "Come down to my house." He took us to the back of his house where there was a deep freezer that was full of meat and fresh vegetables.

He said to us, "Just take anything you want." We took the food home and fixed it ourselves. That pastor and his wife never did feed us or give us one thing to eat the entire time we were there.

They took up an offering every night, but they never gave us any of it, so we couldn't go buy something to eat. Finally the last night of the meeting, they did give us a small offering. I think for the whole week they finally gave us about $43.

We were sorely tempted to get out of love, but I couldn't gripe and complain about it. I've got to walk in love if I'm going to stay healthy. I just like it so much better staying well. So my wife and I just put our faith in God. We knew that down the road God would meet our need, so we just went our way.

What happened to those pastors? Some time later, the district superintendent called me and asked, "Did you preach for those folks?" I told him that I had held a meeting for them at their church.

He asked me, "Did you pick up anything in your spirit while you were there?" I didn't have to pick anything up in my spirit! I mean, if nothing else, going all those days without food, my stomach told me something was wrong!

He said, "We had to deal with those folks. We just had to simply take that church away from them."

I noticed that was the last church that couple ever pastored. The district superintendent had to dismiss them from their fellowship. No one ever heard from them again. In fact, they just disappeared off the scene.

We in the Body of Christ need to treat one another with love! Love works no ill to his neighbor! We can't mistreat people and think we can prosper in the things of God.

I went to hold a meeting for another fellow right here in the state of Oklahoma, and I was glad on that occasion that I went by myself. At that time the children were small, and my wife couldn't travel with me all the time.

This pastor lived in a nice parsonage, and his church was one of the better well-made brick churches in that area.

You have to understand that back in those days, not many Full Gospel churches were made of brick. Some wooden churches existed, but there were very few brick churches. But this pastor's church was one of the nicest churches in this town, and so was his parsonage.

Well, holding a meeting in this church, I had another opportunity to work no ill toward my neighbor. You see, this man gave me accommodations out back behind his parsonage — in his chicken coop!

He hadn't even cleaned it out very well; there were chicken droppings all around. He just put a bed out there, and that's where he put me.

Well, you can imagine how you'd feel about that. And, of course, I've got the flesh to deal with just like you do. My flesh rose up, and I thought, *I don't have to put up with this! I'll just leave.*

But then I realized that I couldn't leave because it might hurt the flock of God. They would wonder why I'd left, and they would have gotten suspicious of their pastor.

You see, love worketh no ill to his neighbor, and God's love in us never takes account of a suffered wrong. So I couldn't do that. I decided to tough it out and stay one week so it wouldn't make the pastor look bad.

I said to the Lord, "Lord, I'll tell You what I'll do. I know the meeting is set up to go longer, but I will finish out the week." In the first meeting, I announced that I'd only preach through Sunday night. I made it look as good on the pastor as I could, and I left on Sunday night.

You ask, "Whatever happened to him?" He died at age 39 with cancer of the throat. That was the last church he ever pastored. In fact, he wasn't even pastoring a church when he died. He was working in a grocery store.

You see, if you don't walk in love, dear friends, you just throw yourself wide open to the devil's attacks.

You'll find out that one reason there is so much sickness in the Body of Christ even among preachers is that believers don't walk in love toward one another. Then people can't get healed until they make adjustments in their heart and begin to walk in love toward one another.

Walking in the love of God is the way to prosper in life. The God-kind of love will bring you into victory in every area of your life. Just endeavor to do what the Bible says and exercise the God-kind of love. You can't prosper in God if you don't treat other people right or if you're holding on to grudges in your heart.

I've trained myself through the years to think like this: "How is what I'm about to say or do going to affect the other fellow? Love worketh no ill to anyone. Is what I'm about to say or do going to hurt the other person? If it is, then I can't say it or do it."

Now don't misunderstand me. I'm far from perfect. I've missed it. But when I saw that I missed it in the love walk, as fast as I could, I repented and got right back walking in the love of God.

Love Works No Ill in Marriage

The God-kind of love works no ill to his neighbor. Well, that applies to husbands and wives too. So if you're married, that includes working ill to your spouse, doesn't it? Therefore, if you're going to walk in the God-kind of love that means you can't work any ill to your husband or to your wife.

When couples are having problems in their marriage, husbands need to ask themselves, "What would love do?" Wives need to ask themselves, "What would love do?"

I'm talking about divine love, not human love. Human love is fickle. You can't walk by human love and be a successful Christian. Human love is just a little bit more than physical attraction.

A woman once asked me if she could talk to me. She said, "It seems like I just don't love my husband anymore."

"What do you mean," I asked, "you don't love your husband anymore?"

"Oh, he's a fine man, and he's good to me. In fact, he's just a wonderful person. But I just don't seem to love him anymore."

You see, she needed to get her mind renewed with the Word of God. I began to talk to her about the love of God and to teach her how to develop God's love so it could grow and increase.

Finally I said, "Why don't you let God's love dominate you? God's love will solve every problem that comes up."

You see, if you walk in the God-kind of love, you'll succeed every time because God's love bears up under anything and everything that comes. We have the God-kind of love in us! We can love like God loves.

If we'll just listen to the Bible and make the love of God our great quest and develop the love of God on the inside, we'll prosper in every area of life.

Husbands and wives need to let the love of God dominate them — not just natural, human love. Naturally, husbands and wives have a certain amount of physical affection and attraction toward each other. But natural love is so shallow. It can turn to hatred overnight.

The love of God won't do that. And, you see, Christians have the advantage over other folks.

Not only can they love their husband or wife with natural affection, but they can also add this divine love to their natural affection for each other. They can love each other with the God-kind of love, which never seeks its own, but always seeks the other's welfare.

Couples need to practice seeking their spouses' welfare before they seek their own. Couples who do this would experience Heaven on earth in their marriages.

Even in marriage, put the other person first. Think to yourself, *How can I be a blessing to my spouse.* Think of the other person's welfare before your own.

Some folks don't do that, and it creates problems in their marriage. For example, some dear women, bless their hearts, get so "spiritual" they think they are too holy to have sexual relations with their husband. But this verse, "Love works no ill to anyone," applies to them too.

They couldn't be exercising this verse toward their husband. Are they working any ill to their husband by not being a wife to him? Absolutely! They're liable to cause him to stumble and fall into sin, and then they would have to share in the blame for it.

Some of them say, "Yes, but God told me not to have physical relations with my husband."

If He did, then He lied in His Word because His Word said that married couples are not to defraud one another.

1 CORINTHIANS 7:5
5 **DEFRAUD YE NOT ONE THE OTHER,** except it be with consent for a time, that ye may give

yourselves to fasting and prayer; and come together again, that Satan tempt you not for your incontinency.

The Bible says that a husband and a wife are not to defraud one another. What does that mean? *Moffatt's* translation says, "Do not withhold sexual intercourse from one another, unless you agree to do so for a time. . . ."

In other words, if both husband and wife agree to it, they can withhold sexual relations for a time so "they can give themselves to fasting and prayer."

But then *Moffatt's* translation says, "Then come together again." That means to come together and resume marital relations again. You see, walking in love has to do with every part of our lives, even in married life.

The Bible tells married people exactly how to treat their own wife or husband. I mean the Bible covers every area of our lives.

My wife and I were holding a meeting for a pastor years ago, and every time you asked him a question, he'd say, "I'll have to ask my wife." It seemed like she just had total control over him in every area.

We held a three-week meeting for this pastor, and then we had a week off.

This pastor said to me, "Brother Hagin, my wife and I are going to the mountains. Why don't you and your wife come and join us?" We had free time, so we went with them.

During that time, he told me, "Brother Hagin, I sometimes go for four months at a time, and my wife never lets me sleep with her. But she loves to go to the mountains. So the only way I can get her to have sexual relations with me is to take her to the mountains."

That fellow was only a little bit older than I was at the time, and I was only about thirty years old.

By withholding marital relations from him, that pastor's wife could have caused this pastor to stumble. Then some people would have said, "Look what that dirty Pentecostal preacher did!"

But if he had stumbled, his wife would have been mostly to blame for it. Love worketh no ill or evil to anyone. This wife worked evil to her husband.

In fact, that wife violated the Word of God. It couldn't have been God who told her not to have relations with her husband because the Word said, *"Defraud ye not one the other"* (1 Cor. 7:5).

The love of God will work in every area of life, including in the marriage relationship. Husbands and wives need to ask themselves, *What would love do?*

And if each one of us wants to grow and develop in the God-kind of love, then before we respond to people, we need to ask ourselves the questions, *How would God's love act? What would God's love do?*

This is the way we can get the God-kind of love to abound in our lives! The love of God never fails, so when you put the love of God to work in your life, you will never fail.

Make this confession from your heart:

The love of God has been shed abroad in my heart by the Holy Ghost. I shall endeavor to let that love nature dominate me. I have God's love nature in my heart — in my spirit.

Therefore, I'll not let my natural human reasoning dominate me. I refuse to allow the flesh to rule me.

I'm going to walk in the Spirit by walking in love. I am a lover, not a hater.

I will practice and exercise the fruit of love so that it can grow and increase.

One way I will practice the God-kind of love is by taking no thought for a suffered wrong.

I will also practice thinking the best of every person so my love can grow and develop, and I can be a blessing to many.

I will make the love of God my great quest in life, for then my love shall abound, and God shall reap the glory.

Chapter 2

Divine Love:
The Evidence of the New Birth

Many people think the evidence of their salvation rests in the fact that they have joined a certain church. Or they think that because they've been water baptized a certain way with a certain formula, they are on their way to Heaven.

For example, sometimes you hear people say, "You've got to belong to *my* church or you're not saved." Or "You've got to be baptized according to *our* formula, or you're not saved. You won't get to Heaven."

But what does the Bible say is the evidence of the new birth? According to the Bible, we know we are saved because we confess Jesus Christ as our Lord (Rom. 10:9,10). Then the Bible also says that we know we are saved because we *love* the brethren.

> **1 JOHN 3:14**
> **14 WE KNOW that we have passed from death unto life, BECAUSE WE LOVE THE BRETHREN. . . .**

I like this verse: *"WE KNOW that we have passed from death unto life. . . ."* That's positive, isn't it? This

45

verse doesn't read, "We *think* we have passed from death unto life. . . ." It doesn't read, "This is my *opinion* or *theory*" or "This is the way I have it *figured out*."

No, the apostle says, "We *know* we have passed from spiritual death unto eternal life because we *love* the brethren."

When John said, ". . . *we have passed from death unto life. . . ,*" he isn't talking about physical death here. We haven't passed from physical death yet. The day is coming when physical death will be put underfoot. It is the last enemy to be dealt with, but it hasn't been put underfoot yet.

No, by using the word "death" here, John is talking about spiritual death, which is the separation of the human spirit from God. Therefore, we can read this verse like this: We *know* we've passed from spiritual death and its consequences — eternal separation from God — to *eternal* life because we have this fruit called love.

In the new birth we are born of the Spirit of God, and that's when the love of God comes into our hearts. When we were born again spiritually, we partook of God's life and God's love. Eternal life is the life of God imparted into our spirits.

In our natural birth we partake of the life and nature of our parents. When we are born of God, we partake of God's nature. God's nature is *life* and *love*. The love of God is shed abroad in our hearts, and we receive eternal life.

The Bible says if we don't love the brethren, we are abiding in spiritual death. Spiritual death is the state we were in before we were born again, when Satan was our spiritual father (Rom. 5:17-21).

The love of God in our hearts is the evidence that we have been translated out of Satan's kingdom of darkness into God's Kingdom of light (Col. 1:13).

When you were born again, you passed from spiritual death to spiritual life. Therefore, you don't have to pray and fast for the God-kind of love so you can love the brethren. If you're saved, you have God's love because it's been shed abroad in your heart by the Holy Spirit.

If you don't have God's love abiding in your heart, you're not saved. It's that simple, because the last part of First John 3:14 says, ". . . *He that loveth not his brother abideth in death.*"

That means if you don't love your brother in Christ, you are still abiding in spiritual death or separation from God.

Of course, what usually happens when believers say they don't love their brethren is that they are looking to their flesh for the love of God, and God's love doesn't dwell in the flesh. No, they will have to look in their heart or spirit for the love of God, and then put God's love to work for them.

The Bible says you know you have passed from death unto life because you love the brethren! If you don't have God's love in your heart, you don't have any evidence of salvation — that is, you don't have the evidence that you've passed from death unto life. Remember, love is the very first fruit that shows up in the new birth.

How We Know We Are Saved

John uses the illustration of passing from death to life as the evidence of the new birth. For example, suppose you were attending a funeral, and right in the middle of the service, the dead person jumped up totally healed and alive. He'd passed from physical death to life.

Now if you ran up to that person and tried to argue with him that he was still dead, he'd just laugh at you. If you said, "Wait a minute! You're dead! You couldn't be alive because you don't belong to our church! You haven't been baptized in water according to the right formula, so you've got to be dead! You're not one of us, so you're dead!"

If you said that to someone who had been brought back from death to life, it wouldn't bother him at all. He knows that he's passed from death to life, and no one could convince him otherwise.

It's the same way with the new birth. We *know* we have passed from spiritual death to eternal life. We were dead in our trespasses and sins, but God quickened us spiritually and made us alive unto Him. We passed from spiritual death to spiritual life.

For example, I knew exactly when I passed from death unto life. I was there! When I was born again and passed from death to life, it was just like a two-ton weight rolled off my chest.

I was born again on the bed of sickness, but after I was healed, I ran into those who told me that I wasn't saved because I didn't belong to their church. I just laughed at them. I said, "I know I've been born again. I know I've passed from death unto life. And I've got the evidence to prove it — I love the brethren!"

I remember a businessman in my hometown who had a stroke and couldn't get around much anymore. His wife had to run the family business. This businessman and his wife never went to church. But about the time he had this stroke, his little nine-year-old daughter got saved and filled with the Holy Ghost and began going to Sunday school and church.

Every day after school when the little girl was outside playing, she'd run into the house every once in a while to check on her daddy and make sure he was all right. Ever since the stroke, he'd been confined to a wheelchair. She would check up on him and ask him, "Daddy, are you all right?"

He'd say, "Yes, Honey, I'm fine," and she'd run back outside and play.

One time she ran into the house and asked him, "Daddy, are you saved? Have you ever been born again?"

Without thinking, he said, "Yes, Honey." And she ran back out to play. But he got to thinking about it and realized that although he'd joined the church forty-nine years before, he had never been born again.

So he called his daughter back in and said, "Honey, I have never lied to you about anything. You asked awhile ago if I was saved.

"Without thinking I said yes because I joined a church. But, really, if I've ever been born again, I don't know it."

She said, "Well, Daddy, you need to get saved because you're old, and if you're not saved, you'll go to hell." And it was true. He could easily have had another stroke and died at any minute.

So the businessman said, "After that, my wife and I decided to start going to church with her." His wife rededicated her life to the Lord, and he got saved. Then in the process of time, he and his wife were both filled with the Holy Ghost.

Well, after this man got baptized in the Holy Spirit, he was also miraculously healed. I mean, he was up walking just as good as anyone.

I went to visit him, and he told me that he got so many telephone calls and letters about his healing that he just took out a half-page ad in the newspaper and told everyone about Jesus healing him!

One day when I was back visiting that church, I went by to see him. He began telling me about his salvation experience. One night during a revival meeting, a visiting evangelist had asked him, "Are you saved?"

He answered, "Yes, sir, I am."

The evangelist asked, "How do you know you are saved?"

"Well," he said, "I'll tell you how I know I'm saved. I've been going to this church for three years now, and every Wednesday night we have a testimony meeting.

"And you could always count on the fact that the first one up to testify would be old man Smith. He's just an old codger, and he'd always testify and double up his fist, and say, 'I'm saved and sanctified!' like he was challenging folks. I'd get so mad, I'd sit there and quietly cuss at him under my breath.

"I'd say to myself, *Old man, if I weren't crippled like this, I'd just see how sanctified you are!*

"Then you could always count on it, the very next one up to testify would be old lady Bailey. And as she testified, I'd sit there and criticize her too.

"I'd say to myself, 'That old woman is always out trying to get everyone saved. But when her husband comes home, the beds aren't made and the house is a mess. Her kids are out running up and down back alleys, and she hasn't even made supper for her family.'

"I just knew that old lady didn't have anything. If she did, her family wouldn't be in such a mess. Every time she testified, and the more I thought about her, the madder I'd get, until I'd just sit there cursing under my breath."

But then this businessman said something interesting. He said, "But then the Lord saved me, and my heart changed. Ever since then, I just dearly love to hear old Brother Smith testify." (Before he'd called him old man Smith.)

"Oh, I know he's a little eccentric, but he loves the Lord. And I'll tell you, now that I'm saved, I love to hear dear Sister Bailey testify too." (Before he'd called her old lady Bailey.)

"I know, of course, that she may not be a hundred-percent perfect, but then, not one of us is. But right on the other hand, I know her husband, because he used to work for me. And he was the type of fellow who was difficult to please and impossible to live with.

"In fact, he would tell me, 'I'm going to go home, and if my wife hasn't got supper on the table, I'm going to get mad and cuss her out. And if she does have dinner on the table, I'm going to knock it off on the floor.'

"Well, naturally she made sure she was gone when he got home. But since I've been saved, I just love to hear dear Sister Bailey testify."

You see, this man knew he had passed from death to life because he loved the brethren! When the love of God was shed abroad in his heart, it made all the difference because now he loved the brethren.

But, you see, one thing we've got to realize is that the Holy Spirit can be in your heart in the new birth, but if you don't allow the love of God to dominate you, you'll just walk on in carnality and be defeated.

Just as a side thought, in the course of time, Sister Bailey got all of her children and her husband saved. When I went back to visit that church, the whole family was sitting on the pew worshipping God together.

But how did this businessman know he was saved? He knew he had passed from spiritual death — and its consequence of eternal separation from God — to life because now he loved the brethren!

The Love of God Constrains Us

When you're born again, and you've passed from spiritual death to eternal life, the love of God that has been shed abroad in your heart will constrain you to do what's right in God's sight.

> **2 CORINTHIANS 5:14**
> **14 For the love of Christ constraineth us. . . .**

God's love can transform and change the hardest heart. And when you allow the love of God to constrain you, you won't act like you did before you got saved.

I remember when I was born again in 1933, there was a change on the inside of me. I became a new creature. Old things in my spirit passed away, and I was a different person. When you're born again, your spiritual nature is completely changed.

Before I was saved, I didn't have the love of God shed abroad in my heart. My daddy left us when I was six years old, and I don't really remember too much in connection with him.

In fact, I have to think real hard to remember three or four incidents about him because he was never there.

He would just go and stay gone for long periods of time. Finally, he left home and never did come back.

So I grew up in a broken home, and because of it, I was mad at the whole world. When I was nine years old, I went to live with my grandparents. My oldest brother went to live with our other grandparents. We children were scattered, and I was brought up as an orphan boy, kicked from pillar to post.

Not only was our home broken, but I was always sickly as a child. I couldn't run and play like other children. I couldn't stick up for myself — even the girls could whip me. I had a chip on my shoulder because I didn't think I'd gotten a fair deal in life.

My oldest brother, Dub, and I made a pact that when we got grown, we were going to kill our daddy. And I'll tell you, the only thing that kept us from doing it was getting saved. We fully intended to do it.

I found out in the second grade that if I was going to make it in life, I had to find an equalizer — something to do my fighting for me — because I was small and physically afflicted and sickly. I couldn't protect myself or fight because I had a heart condition. If I tried to exert myself the least bit, I would just pass out.

For example, in the second grade, a bully who was three years older than me hit me in the face and knocked me down. I should have had enough sense to just lie there, but I got up and made an effort to fight him, so he knocked me down again.

I got up, and he knocked me down again, and I passed out. I was unconscious about an hour and a half. The school nurse later told me, "You turned black-and-blue all over. We didn't think you were ever going to come out of it."

Not only was I small and sickly, but the kids in school picked on me and tried to torment me a lot. Since my dad had left us, the kids in school would get to talking, and they'd tell everyone I was illegitimate.

They'd get to talking about their daddies. Well, I couldn't talk about my daddy because I didn't know anything about him.

When they weren't calling me names, they were taunting me, saying that my dad was gone because he was in the penitentiary. That would make me mad, and I'd want to fight, but I'd always pass out when I exerted myself. I had to prove to those fellows that I could take care of myself so they wouldn't bother me.

You understand that I wasn't a Christian yet. My old flesh nature dominated me. Well, since I couldn't protect myself, I decided to use a short two-by-four that I could handle to be my equalizer to do my fighting for me. Then I would slip up behind anyone who did me wrong and knock him in the head.

I did that a couple times, and the kids started leaving me alone. Word got around. But somehow or another when you're an orphan boy and you don't have any daddy, and you're sickly, afflicted, and can't fight, the other kids want to whip you. I guess they think it proves how big they are.

My older brother, Dub, used to tease me because I was so small and sickly. He'd tell me, "When you're twelve years old, you're going to turn into a girl." He'd say that, and then he'd take off running, because he knew if I caught him, I'd hit him with whatever I could find.

Before I was born again, when someone did me wrong, I'd make a mental note of it. I wouldn't do anything about it just then. I'd wait until the person wasn't looking, and I'd slip up behind him and knock him in the head with a brick or a two-by-four.

You see, I grew up twisted because my daddy had left us to get along any way we could. I can understand how some folks today are twisted because they grew up in similar circumstances. I know what it's like to be pushed and knocked around and cussed at.

When you're in the natural, you want to retaliate. The only cure for that is to get born again so the love of God will be shed abroad in your heart. When you get the love of God in you, it changes you. And if you are born again, you've got to let the love of God dominate you.

Before I was a new creature, if any of my kinfolks wronged me in any way, I would make a mental note of it, and I'd mark them off my list and never speak to them again. And after that, even if they were in the same room, I'd just ignore them like they didn't exist.

Or if someone had wronged me, and I saw him walking down the street, I'd cross the street in the middle of the block to avoid speaking to him.

But then I was born again. Immediately there was a change inside me. My nature was changed. The love of God was shed abroad in my heart! I didn't really know what all had happened to me. I just knew I was born again and that I was a new creature. I knew that the inward man had changed and that I had passed from spiritual death unto life.

I was bedfast at the time, but then the next year I got healed and was raised up from a deathbed.

Shortly after my healing, one of my relatives told a lie about me. Without thinking, I just said to myself, *I'll give her the old treatment and mark her off my list. I won't speak to her again the longest day I live.*

You see, even though I was born again, my mind wasn't thoroughly renewed with the Word of God yet, so my old carnal thinking still dominated me. I hadn't read Ephesians 4:23 yet. I didn't know that the love of God had been shed abroad in my heart. I just knew that I was born again and that I had changed on the inside.

But just because our spirits were recreated doesn't mean our bodies and our minds were changed. No, our bodies and our minds aren't born again. We have the same carnal body and mind we had before we were born again.

Soon after I was healed and up walking around, I saw this relative that had told a lie about me coming down the street toward me. The thought flashed into my mind to give her the old treatment, so I started to cross the street to keep from meeting her. But something in my heart rose up on the inside of me and constrained me not to do that.

You see, the Bible says that we *know* that we have passed from death unto life because the love of God has been shed abroad in our heart by the Holy Ghost. What is it we *know*? That we have passed from spiritual death unto life because we love the brethren!

So down on the inside, the love of God constrained me. Instead of turning my back on this relative, the love of God rose up inside me, and I just began to weep because I felt so sorry for her.

I said to myself, "That dear one, bless her heart. She can't help but act that way because she's unsaved and a child of the devil. Children of the devil act like the devil. Children of God act like God. I've passed from death unto life, but she's still in spiritual death, and spiritual death dominates her."

So instead of turning my back on her, I went to meet her. I put my hand out, shook hands with her and said, "I just want you to know that I love you. And I want you to know that if it would help you in any way at all, I'd just get down on my knees right here on the sidewalk and kiss your feet."

When I said that, my relative started weeping. She put my hand on her head and said, "My God, Ken, pray for me! I need it."

Love never fails! I found out early in my Christian walk I can't let the flesh with its old unrenewed thinking dominate me. I've got to put God's love into action.

The Bible says, "*. . . the love of Christ constraineth us. . .*" (2 Cor. 5:14). What does the love of God on the inside of our hearts constrain us to do? It constrains us to do the right thing — to obey the law of love. Something on the inside in my spirit constrained me to walk in love, and I listened to it.

So instead of avoiding my relative, the Holy Ghost constrained me to go to her, shake her hand, and say, "I want you to know I love you."

When I said that to her, I was speaking out of my recreated heart, not out of my old, carnal thinking. My old unrenewed thinking and my flesh still wanted to retaliate and never speak to her again. The flesh will always want to do what is wrong.

That's why we have to allow the love of God to constrain us. If your mouth is always blabbing off, going a mile a minute, and your flesh is all riled up — it will be easy for the natural man to dominate you. But if you'll just take time to look down on the inside, you'll find that there's something on the inside that's trying to constrain you to act in love.

Look at Paul. He still had the flesh to contend with. But Paul was a great man of God because he allowed the love of God to constrain him. He said, "I keep my body under" (1 Cor. 9:27). Even Paul had to keep the unregenerated desires of his flesh and mind under subjection to his born-again, recreated spirit.

2 CORINTHIANS 5:17
17 Therefore if any man be in Christ, he is a new creature: old things are passed away; behold, all things are become new.

You have to keep the flesh under because all things do *not* become new in your mind or in your body. All things become new in your *spirit*. This verse is talking about all things becoming new in the inward man.

Your body is not the real you. It couldn't be the real you because Paul said that "he" — the man on the inside — did something with his body. Well, what are you supposed to do with your body? You present it to God as a living sacrifice, and you keep it under subjection to your spirit — to the man on the inside.

2 CORINTHIANS 4:16
16 For which cause we faint not; but though our OUTWARD MAN perish, yet THE INWARD MAN is renewed day by day.

When Paul talks about the new creature, he is talking about the inward man — man's spirit. And in the inward man, old things are passed away and all things are become new.

2 CORINTHIANS 5:6
6   Therefore we are always confident, knowing that, whilst we are at HOME IN THE BODY, we are absent from the Lord.

So then the body is the home or the house that the real you — the spirit man on the inside — lives in. But old things haven't passed away in the outward man.

You still have the same body and mind you always had. And your body will want to do the same things it did before you were born again. Your mind will want to think the same thoughts it did before you were saved.

For example, when someone wrongs you, your flesh — your unredeemed nature — wants to retaliate. Your flesh still has that get-even nature: "You hit me, and I'll hit you. You mistreat me, and I'll get even." That's the reason the Bible says we have to keep our flesh under the control of the man on the inside. Our spirit man has to dominate our flesh.

The inward man is to rule and dominate the outward man. That's why we must keep our body under and rule our body; we don't let our body rule us. Even Paul's body wanted to do things that were wrong or he wouldn't have had to keep it under subjection to his spirit.

If you don't know the Bible, the devil will tell you, "You claim to be a Christian, yet you want to do things that are wrong. You couldn't be saved!"

No, you can be thoroughly saved, but your flesh will still want to do what's wrong. That's the reason the Bible tells us to keep our flesh under subjection to the man on the inside.

> **ROMANS 12:1**
> 1   I beseech you therefore, brethren, by the mercies of God, that ye **PRESENT YOUR BODIES A LIVING SACRIFICE,** holy, acceptable unto God, which is your reasonable service.

Some people think that keeping the flesh under just refers to sexual sins. That's a part of keeping the flesh under, of course, but it is only a small part of it. It also means you have to keep your tongue under the control of the inward man that has been born again and created in the image and likeness of God.

For example, some people are prone to talk and gossip about others. They don't realize that when they do that, they are allowing their flesh to rule them.

For instance, Sister Blab-mouth is always saying, "Did you hear the latest? Have you heard what So-and-so is doing?" And then lest you think I'm just picking on women, Brother Blab-mouth is just as bad at gossiping, if not worse!

No, you've got to keep the *whole* body under subjection to your recreated spirit. The Bible says to present your whole body to God as a living sacrifice.

All believers have to keep their flesh under the control of their recreated human spirit, because we still have that old adamic nature in our flesh, even though our spirits have been recreated.

You see, talking about the flesh, there's a beast in all of us. You can't let that beast express itself. You need to keep it under the control of your spirit.

Believers who let their flesh dominate them are carnal Christians. That's why we need to let the love of God constrain us, so we can grow out of the babyhood stage of carnality and become mature believers who walk by the light of the Word.

Mature believers walk in the light of the law of love. God's love shed abroad in our hearts will eventually lead us to victory in life because God's love never fails. The God-kind of love is always victorious.

Learn To Put God's Love To Work for You

Believers who are mature in God's love know how to let the love of God dominate them. They know how to let the love of God work for them.

I remember when Dub was still a baby Christian, he went into town one day to take care of some business for Mamma. When he was in town, he had some problems with some relatives and almost got into a fight with them, so I had to go attend to the business myself.

Dub said, "You'd better not go there. They'll fight you."

I just said, "No, they won't. You just don't know how to exercise the love of God and put it to work for you."

Think about it a minute. How do you put God to work? The Bible said, "God is love." So if you put God's love to work, you're putting God to work in the situation.

The Bible says, *"greater is he that is in you, than he that is in the world"* (1 John 4:4). Well, who is in you? God the Holy Ghost is in you if you've been born again. The Holy Ghost has shed the love of God abroad in your heart. That love in you is bigger than the devil that is in someone who is unsaved and walking in darkness.

So I went to see one of the relatives who had given Dub such a problem, and she just started ranting and raving. I never said a word. I just looked at her, and I felt so sorry for her. I thought to myself, *She can't help but act that way because she's got the nature of the devil in her. She can't help but be selfish.*

But on the inside of me, I just kept saying, "Thank God, the love of God is in me. The love of God in me is bigger than the hatred that is in her. Greater is He who is in me than he that is in her." I just stood there and looked at her in love.

Suddenly she looked at me. Her mouth moved in anger, but nothing came out! She couldn't say one word to me.

She must have seen the expression of love on my face, because all of a sudden, she knelt down on the ground, grabbed my hand and kissed it, and laid it on her head, and said, "Ken, pray for me. You know we all need prayer." So I started praying for her.

Then she called her husband. He said to me, "Some of the relatives are going to try to take everything away from your poor ole Mamma. What are you going to do about it?" I knew he was the one trying to do it.

So I just stepped closer to him, and said, "I want you to know something. I'm ready for any situation. In fact," and I stepped a little closer and dropped my voice and said, "I've got some *inside* information. And I want you to know that I am ready for them."

His countenance changed entirely. He said, "I'll tell you one thing. I'm going to make sure your Mamma gets her share and is provided for." And he did too.

The inside information I had was information inside the Bible. The inside information was "Greater is He that is in me, than he that is in them. Greater is the love of God that is in me than the hatred that is in the world." Love always wins, because the God-kind of love is the way of the New Covenant, and it never fails.

Get inside this Book, the Bible, and get the Bible inside you, and you're ready for anything. You don't have to *get* ready; you *are* ready. God's love never fails!

You Can Mature in Love

Sometimes it takes time and spiritual growth to learn how to put God's love to work for you. We don't grow up spiritually overnight. You can't put an adult head on a baby's body, and sometimes it takes time to mature in love.

My brother Dub was a good example of that. It took him time to mature in love because of his upbringing. Dub was always big for his age. By the time he was sixteen, he was 6 foot 4 inches tall.

But Dub grew up with a chip on his shoulder because he'd been orphaned and kicked from pillar to post. He wouldn't take anything from anyone. In fact, when he was a seventeen-year-old boy, I saw him whip four grown men.

But then Dub got saved. And, really, if you'd known where he'd come from, you would have known that something miraculous happened to him to change his nature. But even though there was a dramatic change on the inside, sometimes he still had a hard time keeping his flesh under. He had to learn to mature in love, and really, he came a long way from his younger days.

But one time, for example, Dub was out in California, and he went into a little coffee shop. He was sitting at the counter, and he ordered something to eat.

When the waitress brought it to him, he bowed his head to pray before he ate. After he prayed, the fellow sitting next to Dub asked him where he was from. Dub said that he was from Oklahoma.

Then the man asked, "Do you know Oral Roberts?"

Dub said, "Well, I don't know him personally, but I've shaken his hand."

Well," the fellow replied, "He's a so-and-so," and he called him a name.

Then the fellow asked, "Do you know Kenneth Copeland?"

"Yes," Dub said. "I know him personally."

"Well," the fellow replied, "he's another so-and-so."

Then the fellow said, "Do you know Kenneth Hagin?"

Dub replied, "Yes, I do."

The fellow said, "He's another so-and-so."

When the fellow said that, Dub knocked him off the counter stool. Then he picked him up and carried him outside.

The owner of the restaurant called the police, and when they got there, Dub was holding the fellow up against the building praying for him.

The police officer said, "What's the matter?"

Dub said, "This man said my brother was a so-and-so. By saying that, he was calling my mother a dirty name too. No one talks that way about my family!"

The policeman said to the fellow, "Did you do that?"

The man said, "Yes."

The policeman said, "Why, you ought to have better sense!" Then he asked Dub, "Who is your brother?"

Dub said, "Kenneth Hagin."

The police officer said, "Oh! I've read his books and listened to his tapes." Then he turned to the other fellow and said, "What's the matter with you!"

The fellow said, "Well, I guess maybe I did do wrong."

My brother Dub told the fellow, "If you want help, here's my card. Come and see me."

The man came to see Dub the next day and got saved!

Now I don't advocate getting people saved that way, but I just told you that to show you that sometimes it can take time to learn to keep the flesh under and to mature in love.

But Dub came a long way from his younger years. It took him a while, but he grew in love.

The Lord had worked Dub over on the inside and made him a new creature, but then Dub had to learn what to do with the outward natural man. It took him some time to learn to put on Christ on the outward man (Rom. 13:14) and to mature in the God-kind of love.

But it's no use laughing at or criticizing Dub, because the Lord is still teaching some of *us* how to put on Christ on the outward man and keep the flesh under too!

I was preaching a sermon in a church I was pastoring in Texas one time. In my sermon I asked the question, "If you were looking for a spiritual person, where would you look?

"Where would you go to see if a person is really spiritual?" A person is only spiritual if he practices walking in God's love.

Some folks said, "I'd go to church to look for someone who is really spiritual." Other folks answered that if someone jumped and hollered and talked in tongues, he must really be spiritual.

I said, "If I were looking for a spiritual person, I wouldn't even go to church, although spiritual people do go to church."

I said, "If I were trying to find a spiritual person, the first place I'd look would be in his home to see how he acts and lives at home."

There was a lady, bless her heart, who sat on the first row in front of the pulpit. When I said this, she said out loud, "Oh, my God! That leaves me out!"

When she said that I nearly fell over the pulpit laughing. Everyone in the church just started laughing right out loud. It just stopped the whole service.

When we finally all regained our composure, I said to the congregation, "Well, at least this lady is a little more honest than some folks."

Bless her heart, that lady was just a baby Christian then, but she did straighten up and become a mature Christian. She grew and developed and matured in her love walk and became a stalwart Christian.

If you don't think you have matured in love yet, don't get discouraged. Just keep on growing in the fruit of love. And by practicing walking in the love of God and by communing with God, it won't be long until you are growing in the God-kind of love!

Chapter 3
Love: The Law
Of the New Covenant

If you are familiar with the Old Testament, you know that under the Old Covenant, the Law refers to the first five Books of the Bible, called the Pentateuch. It can also refer to the Ten Commandments. The Old Testament Law was based on rules and regulations.

People under the Old Covenant were natural men. They weren't born again because Jesus had not yet come and redeemed us by giving His life as a ransom for our sins. He had not yet ushered in the New Covenant with His own blood.

Therefore, people under the Old Covenant had to be dealt with in the natural realm by rules and regulations. They couldn't be led by their heart or spirit because their spirits weren't born again. And under the Old Covenant, if a person broke one point of the Law, he was counted guilty of breaking all the Law.

But under the New Covenant, we are born-again new creatures (2 Cor. 5:17). Because our spirits have been recreated, God has written His law upon our hearts. Therefore, we aren't subject to the Old Testament Law with its rules and regulations, which were meant to control the impulses of natural man.

Under the New Covenant, Jesus gave us a new commandment because we are new creations who are to be led by our recreated spirit or heart. Through the New Birth, our spirits have been recreated by God (2 Cor. 5:17; Eph 4:24). Therefore, we can be led by God through our spirits because that's where the love of God dwells.

> **JOHN 13:34,35**
> **34 A NEW COMMANDMENT I give unto you, THAT YE LOVE ONE ANOTHER; as I have loved you, that YE ALSO LOVE ONE ANOTHER.**
> **35 By this shall all men know that ye are my disciples, IF YE HAVE LOVE ONE TO ANOTHER.**

Under the New Covenant, the law of love is a commandment. God didn't give it to us as a suggestion. Jesus said, *"A new COMMANDMENT I give unto you, That ye love one another. . ."* (John 13:34). Jesus didn't give us a new suggestion or a new idea. He gave us a new commandment.

We know that under the Old Covenant, there were statutes, commandments, and regulations the people had to keep in order to fulfill their part of the covenant. For example, the Old Testament Law included the Ten Commandments (Exod. 20:1-17).

But under the New Covenant, Jesus only gave us one new law or commandment. The new law was to take the place of the old Law. The law of love is the new law. Abiding by the New Testament law of love takes the place of the old Law with its regulations, statutes, and commandments.

There is something else we need to see about the New Covenant law of love. The New Testament commandment of love is a fulfillment of the Ten Commandments. The law of love completed or fulfilled the Old Testament commandments.

The Law of Love
Supersedes the Ten Commandments

The new commandment of love takes the place of the Ten Commandments, because the New Covenant superseded and fulfilled the Old Covenant.

When Jesus fulfilled the Old Covenant, He established a New Covenant in His blood (Heb. 12:24). The Book of Hebrews tells us that the New Covenant is a better covenant, established on better promises (Heb. 8:6).

You see, you can't live in the Old Testament under its covenant and be a successful Christian, because that covenant was for spiritually dead men who hadn't been born again. Besides, the Old Covenant has been superseded by a new and better covenant. You need to come into the New Covenant and find out what God is saying to you as a born-again believer — as one whose spirit man has been recreated by God (2 Cor. 5:17).

The epistles are the letters that are written to the Church — to you and me. So if you want to find out what God is saying to you, read those Books in the Bible that were written directly to you.

Under the New Covenant, what was the new law Jesus gave us? It is contained in one commandment: *"A NEW COMMANDMENT I give unto you, THAT YE LOVE ONE ANOTHER; as I have loved you, that ye also LOVE ONE ANOTHER"* (John 13:34).

Now when you say that, immediately people ask, "You mean we don't have to keep the Ten Commandments?" You see, many folks have been so religiously brainwashed that they miss what the Bible is saying about the new commandment of love.

Well, for those of us who are in Christ, there is no longer any need for us to try to obey each one of the Ten Commandments. Why? Because if we walk in the new commandment of love, we will be fulfilling *all* the commandments of the Old Testament.

That fact is made clear in the Book of Romans. Paul said it this way: "He who loves his neighbor has fulfilled the Law."

> **ROMANS 13:8-10**
> **8** Owe no man any thing, but to love one another: for HE THAT LOVETH ANOTHER HATH FULFILLED THE LAW.
> **9** For this, Thou shalt not commit adultery, Thou shalt not kill, Thou shalt not steal, Thou shalt not bear false witness, Thou shalt not covet; and IF THERE BE ANY OTHER COMMANDMENT, IT IS BRIEFLY COMPREHENDED IN THIS SAYING, namely, THOU SHALT LOVE THY NEIGHBOUR AS THYSELF.

**10 Love worketh no ill to his neighbour: THERE-
FORE LOVE IS THE FULFILLING OF THE LAW.**

Here the Bible says that if we love one another, we
have fulfilled the Old Testament Law with all of its
ordinances, statutes, and commandments. If you walk
in love, you don't need any other commandments.

The Bible says, ". . . *In the mouth of two or three
witnesses shall every word be established*" (2 Cor. 13:1).
Let me give you three New Testament witnesses that
prove the New Testament law of love supersedes or fulfills the Ten Commandments under the Old Covenant.

We read in Hebrews that the New Covenant of love
is to be written in our hearts.

HEBREWS 8:7-13
**7   For if that FIRST COVENANT had been fault-
less, then should no place have been sought for the
SECOND** [covenant].
**8   For finding fault with them, he saith, Behold,
the days come, saith the Lord, when I will make A
NEW COVENANT with the house of Israel and
with the house of Judah:**
**9   Not according to the covenant that I made with
their fathers in the day when I took them by the
hand to lead them out of the land of Egypt;
because they continued not in my covenant, and I
regarded them not, saith the Lord.**
**10   For THIS IS THE COVENANT that I will make
with the house of Israel after those days, saith the
Lord; I will put my laws into their mind, AND
WRITE THEM IN THEIR HEARTS: and I will be to
them a God, and they shall be to me a people:**
**11   And they shall not teach every man his neigh-
bour, and every man his brother, saying, Know the**

> **Lord: for all shall know me, from the least to the greatest.**
> **12 For I will be merciful to their unrighteousness, and their sins and their iniquities will I remember no more.**
> **13 In that he saith, A NEW COVENANT, HE HATH MADE THE FIRST OLD. Now that which decayeth and waxeth old IS READY TO VANISH AWAY.**

This Scripture states that God would give us a new commandment, which He would write in our hearts. It says this new commandment of love would fulfill or make the first covenant with its Old Testament commandments old or obsolete. In other words, the Old Covenant would be superseded by the New Covenant.

Now let's see what Jesus said about the new commandment of love. Here is another scriptural witness that under the New Covenant, the new commandment of love is written in our hearts and minds. And it takes the place of the Ten Commandments of the Old Covenant.

> **HEBREWS 10:7-10,14-17**
> **7   Then said I [Jesus], Lo, I come (in the volume of the book it is written of me,) to do thy will, O God.**
> **8   Above when he said, Sacrifice and offering and burnt offerings and offering for sin thou wouldest not, neither hadst pleasure therein; which are offered by THE LAW;**
> **9   Then said he, Lo, I come to do thy will, O God. HE TAKETH AWAY THE FIRST [covenant], that HE MAY ESTABLISH THE SECOND [covenant].**
> **10 By the which will we are sanctified through the offering of the body of Jesus Christ once for all. . . .**

14 For by one offering he hath perfected for ever them that are sanctified.
15 Whereof the Holy Ghost also is a witness to us: for after that he had said before,
16 THIS IS THE COVENANT that I will make with them after those days, saith the Lord, I WILL PUT MY LAWS INTO THEIR HEARTS, and IN THEIR MINDS WILL I WRITE THEM;
17 And THEIR SINS AND INIQUITIES WILL I REMEMBER NO MORE.

Under the Old Covenant, the word "commandment" is in the plural: commandments. But under the New Covenant, the word "commandment" is singular because there is only one commandment, and it is the law of love. And that commandment is written in our recreated spirit or heart.

Remember, Hebrews 8:10 said, *"For this is the covenant that I will make with the house of Israel after those days, saith the Lord; I will put my laws into their minds, and write them in their hearts."*

If the law of love is written in your heart and you're walking in the light of God's love, you are not going to break any of the Ten Commandments. You see, the commandments of the Old Testament were given to curb sin. But if you're walking in love, you're not going to break any of God's commandments.

If you're walking in love, you won't tell a lie about anyone or steal from anyone, will you? No! If you're walking in love, you're not going to kill anyone. If you're walking in love, you're not going to work any ill against your neighbor.

Therefore, when you walk in love, you don't have to try to obey all the laws and commandments of the Old Testament. All you have to do is abide in the one new commandment Jesus gave us — the law of love — and walk in it.

The New Testament also calls the law of love "the royal law" because it is based on the divine love of God.

> **JAMES 2:8,9**
> **8   If ye fulfil THE ROYAL LAW according to the Scripture, THOU SHALT LOVE THY NEIGHBOUR AS THYSELF, ye do well:**
> **9   But if ye have respect to persons, ye commit sin, and are convinced of the law as transgressors.**

According to the Bible, what is the royal law? It says what it is right here: "Thou shalt love thy neighbour as thyself." The law of love is the royal law because it is based on the God-kind of love.

If you're walking in love, no one has to write a commandment to you that says, "Don't lie about So-and-so or steal from him." If you are keeping the New Covenant law of love, you wouldn't want to steal from anyone or lie about anyone because the love of God dwells in your recreated heart or spirit.

I sometimes say it this way: Because the love of God dwells in my heart, I don't have to be concerned about wanting to steal or lie. In fact, I'm stealing all I want to steal, and I'm telling all the lies I want to tell because the "want to" just isn't there!

That reminds me of the story D. L. Moody once told along this line. A young woman came to see him, and she said, "I want to become a Christian, but I just love to dance. I tried to give up dancing to become a Christian, but I just can't." She was talking about worldly dancing, of course.

Mr. Moody said to her, "Why, little lady, just give your heart to Jesus, and you can dance all you want to." Well, that convinced her, so she gave her heart to the Lord and was born again.

A number of days later Mr. Moody said that this young lady met him on the street. She smiled and said, "Mr. Moody, I see what you mean now. The 'want to' is gone!"

Now we may get tripped up from time to time in the flesh since it hasn't been redeemed yet or through our mind if we haven't taken time to renew it.

But if you are really born again, the "want to" to sin is gone. You may stumble in your flesh sometimes, but the "want to" in your spirit is gone!

Another interesting thing about the love of God is that it abides in the heart of man, not in his mind or body.

Why does God's love abide in the heart of man? Because the heart of man is the only part of man that has been recreated.

Go back to the Old Testament and see something Ezekiel prophesied concerning man's heart under the New Covenant.

EZEKIEL 11:19
19 And I will give them one heart, and I WILL
PUT A NEW SPIRIT [heart] **WITHIN YOU; and I**
will TAKE THE STONY HEART OUT of their flesh,
and will give them AN HEART OF FLESH.

You see, under the Old Covenant it was prophesied
that the day was coming when God would take out our
old stony heart and put in a new tender heart of love.

EZEKIEL 36:25-28
25 Then will I sprinkle clean water upon you, and
ye shall be clean: from all your filthiness, and from
all your idols, will I cleanse you.
26 A NEW HEART also will I give you, and a NEW
SPIRIT will I put within you: and I will take away
the STONY HEART out of your flesh, and I will
give you an HEART OF FLESH.
27 And I will put MY SPIRIT within you, and
cause you to walk in my statutes, and ye shall
keep my judgments, and do them.
28 And ye shall dwell in the land that I gave to
your fathers; and ye shall be my people, and I will
be your God.

These verses clearly point to a blessing that is in
store for the Jews (v. 28). God promised that they would
dwell in the land which God gave to their fathers. He
promised that the Jews would be His people, and He
would be their God.

However, there is also an application of these verses
to the Church of the Lord Jesus Christ. This Scripture
is looking forward to the New Covenant when the heart

of man would be changed and recreated in the new birth.

> **2 CORINTHIANS 5:17**
> **17 Therefore if any man be in Christ, he is a NEW CREATURE: old things are passed away; behold, all things are become new** [in his spirit].

Jeremiah also prophesied about the New Covenant that was to come and the change that was to come about in man's heart in the new birth.

> **JEREMIAH 31:33,34**
> **33 But this shall be the covenant that I will make with the house of Israel; After those days, saith the Lord, I WILL PUT MY LAW IN THEIR INWARD PARTS, and write it IN THEIR HEARTS; and will be their God, and they shall be my people.**
> **34 And they shall teach no more every man his neighbour, and every man his brother, saying, Know the Lord: for they shall all know me, from the least of them unto the greatest of them, saith the Lord: for I will forgive their iniquity, and I will remember their sin no more.**

These verses of Scripture refer to the Church — the Body of Christ. How do we know they apply to the Church? Because the writer of the Book of Hebrews quoted these verses in reference to the Church.

> **HEBREWS 8:10**
> **10 For THIS IS THE COVENANT that I will make with the house of Israel after those days, saith the**

**Lord; I WILL PUT MY LAWS INTO THEIR MIND,
and WRITE THEM IN THEIR HEARTS: and I will
be to them a God, and they shall be to me a people.**

In this verse, the writer of the Book of Hebrews is
quoting the Old Testament Scripture in Jeremiah
31:33,34. And he is looking ahead to a time when God
would make a New Covenant whereby the hearts of
men would be changed. Under the New Covenant, it is
the heart or spirit of man that is changed.

But I want you to notice that God also said, "I will
put My laws into their mind." It's God's laws in our
mind that renew or transform our thinking.

The Worrell New Testament says, ". . . Putting My
laws into their mind, I will also write them upon their
hearts. . . ." God expects us to do something with our
minds. We are to renew our minds with His Word, so
our minds can be in agreement with the Holy Spirit
who dwells in our hearts. Once our minds are renewed,
our minds and our hearts will be in agreement with
God's Word.

Because man's heart has been changed under the
New Covenant and he's been given a new heart, there is
a new commandment given for the New Covenant. And
under the New Covenant, God Himself will write the
new commandment of love or the new law of the God-
kind of love in our hearts or spirits.

ROMANS 5:5
**5 . . . THE LOVE OF GOD is shed abroad IN OUR
HEARTS BY THE HOLY GHOST which is given unto us.**

Where is the love of God shed abroad? In our hearts. You see, under the Old Covenant, God wrote the Ten Commandments on tables of stone with His finger, the finger of God (Exod. 24:12; 31:18). You understand that when the Bible talks about "the finger of God," it is referring to the Holy Ghost.

Under the Old Covenant, people's hearts hadn't been born again. In that sense their hearts were stony or unregenerated. Therefore, the love of God couldn't be shed abroad in their hearts by the Holy Ghost. But under the New Covenant, our hearts have been recreated in the new birth and changed from stony hearts to hearts of flesh.

Under the New Covenant, God didn't write His new commandment of love on tables of stone. By the finger of God, the Holy Ghost, God wrote one commandment in our born-again heart or spirit. The commandment He wrote in our heart was that we love one another, because that one commandment fulfills all the other commandments of the Old Testament.

Under the Old Covenant, the Law couldn't make anyone perfect. The blood of bulls and goats could only *atone for* or *cover over* the sins of the Israelites who were not born again.

But Jesus had a more excellent ministry than Moses did. God gave the Law to Moses, but Jesus ushered in a New Covenant in His own blood. Jesus ushered in a better covenant than Moses did because it was established on better promises, and it was ratified with Jesus' own blood.

And by the blood of the Lord Jesus Christ, when we are born again and our hearts are recreated, our sins are not only atoned for, they are remitted, cleansed, or blotted out. That's why God could write the law of love on our hearts because our hearts have been cleansed and recreated.

What kind of love has been shed abroad in our hearts? Is it natural, human love? No, it's the kind of love that God is because God is love.

Why Believers Can Be Led by Their Heart

There is a reason believers can be led by their heart or spirit. In the new birth, the spirit is the part of man that has been recreated by the Holy Ghost.

Under the New Covenant we are told, *"The Spirit itself* [Himself] *beareth witness with our SPIRIT* [heart], *that we are the children of God"* (Rom. 8:16). The Bible says we are to be led by our heart or spirit by the Holy Spirit who lives within us (Rom. 8:14; John 14:16,23).

Every believer needs to learn to listen to his recreated heart or spirit because that's where the law of love is written! God said, "I will write my law in their hearts."

The love of God is shed abroad in our hearts — in the inward man! That's why we can be led by the Holy Spirit in our heart because that's where we've been made a new creation.

God didn't say the love of God would be shed abroad in our heads. That is where people get into trouble. They try to be led by their head — their unrenewed carnal thinking — and their head gets them into trouble.

Many times believers' mental reasoning is cluttered up with religious, carnal thinking because they've never taken time to renew their minds. In fact, many times our spirit or heart suffers at the expense of our head — our carnal thinking. That is the reason we need to get into the Word for ourselves and get our minds renewed with the Word.

It's the same way with the flesh. We can't be led by our flesh either, because our flesh has not been redeemed. No, our flesh is unsanctified and unsaved. Our unredeemed flesh will get us into trouble.

The flesh is not a sure guide because the love of God has not been shed abroad in our flesh. That's why the Bible tells us to keep our flesh under subjection to our born-again, recreated spirit because our spirit has been redeemed.

Really, if we would listen to our heart, we would know in every situation on the inside of us what we ought to do. But so many times our head is all cluttered up with religious teaching instead of our mind being renewed with the Word of God. And it hinders our faith.

Why? Because faith is not of the head. The God-kind of faith is of the heart or spirit of man where the love of God dwells.

Then how can the love of God be activated to its fullest measure? By letting the love of God dominate you, so your faith can grow and reach its full potential. In fact, to tell you the real truth about the matter, understanding how to walk in the God-kind of love is one of the most important subjects you can learn so you can know how to put your faith to work.

A lot of times people concentrate all their thinking on faith, and that is good to a certain extent. But there may be nothing wrong with their faith. Their faith could even be developed, but maybe it's just not activated or working. Faith won't work if there's something wrong with your love walk.

The problem with a lot of folks is that they try to substitute natural human love for divine love, and they're not the same. Then their faith won't work and they don't know why.

Actually, you can't really teach about the faith of God without teaching about the love of God because faith only works by love.

A lot of folks like to hear about faith, but they don't care too much to hear about walking in God's love. But often it's a lack of walking in love that hinders their faith from working.

Love — Faith's Power

Let me give you an example of what I mean. You could have an orchestra with musical instruments and a sound system, but if you don't have any electrical power, the sound won't be amplified. The sound would be ineffectual.

It's the same way with faith and confession. Faith and all the right confessions may be in place, but faith just won't work when there's no power flowing through it. The God-kind of love is the power to faith.

I sometimes tell about the woman who came up to me after a convention a number of years ago. She said, "Brother Hagin, I want you to promise me something."

"Well, what is it? I'm not going to promise until you tell me what it is."

Then she tuned up and began to bawl a little bit. I'm not making fun of her; I'm just stating facts.

She said, "I'm a widow, and I have a fifteen-year-old son. He wasn't raised up in church because I've only been a Christian for the last three years. Well, he's just wild, and I can't do a thing in the world with him. He's out late at night until three and four o'clock in the morning.

"I just lie in bed waiting for the phone to ring and for the authorities to call telling me that he's been arrested because he's into drugs and different things. I want you to promise me that you'll pray for him every day."

I said to her, "I'm not going to do it! I'm not going to make a promise like that because from all probability, I'd never remember to pray for him every day."

"Well, then just pray for him when it comes to you."

I said, "I'm not even going to pray for him at all." I said that to get her attention. She looked at me and blinked like a frog in a west Texas hail storm.

"You're not?" she asked.

"No, I'm not. I'm not going to pray one single prayer for him."

"You're not?"

"No, I'm not." I continued, "It wouldn't do any good for me to pray for him as long as you keep on going the way you're going."

She said, "What do you mean?"

I said, "As long as you keep condemning him, my praying wouldn't do any good. I daresay that you're on him all the time, constantly trying to poke religion down him and trying to push Jesus off on him."

"How do you know I'm that way?"

"Because of the way he turned out," I said. "You've turned him off to God. No, you promise me something. From this day forward, don't say one more word to him about Jesus. And don't keep getting after him all the time."

I continued, "Don't even get after him to go to church. Don't say one word to him about religion, the Bible, church, Jesus, or anything. Just act in love toward him."

Then I said, "And when he's out at night, quit lying there worrying. Instead just say, 'Lord, I surround him with faith and love.'"

You see, faith doesn't work without love. This woman was short-circuiting her own faith because she wasn't walking in love toward her son. She only spoke negatively about him; she didn't speak anything positive or say anything about him that demonstrated the God-kind of love.

I told her, "Just say, 'I surround him with faith and love. I don't believe he's going to wind up in jail. I believe he's going to serve God.'"

She said, "But I don't know whether I believe that or not."

I said, "Start believing it! And if you'll just start saying it, eventually you'll start believing it. Then go on to sleep and forget it. Just leave him alone."

"Well, I'll try," she said.

"It won't work by trying," I said. "It only works by doing it!"

"All right. Then I'll do it. But you're still going to pray for him, aren't you?"

"No," I said, "I'm not going to pray for him. You're going to do it."

You see, this woman's problem was that she hadn't put any action to her faith. Her wrong believing, wrong thinking, and wrong speaking had hindered her faith. Love is the action that motivates faith. Love gives faith its power.

About fifteen months later, I was in the same area teaching at a convention. A woman came up to me after the service. She said, "Do you remember me?"

I said, "No, ma'am, I don't. I see a lot of folks."

"Well, about fifteen months ago you came here, and I asked you pray every day for my son."

"Oh, I remember. But I didn't recognize you! You look so different." Actually, she looked so much younger and prettier.

She said, "Well, I went home, and I did just what you said. I want to tell you — it was tough on me! But I did it. And do you know what?"

"What?" I asked.

"About six months ago, my son came home at four o'clock in the morning on a Saturday night.

Well, I got up the next morning when I usually do and started fixing breakfast because I was going to Sunday school and church.

"My son got up and ate breakfast with me, and said, 'Mom, I believe I'll go with you to Sunday school and church this morning.'

"On the inside of me something was turning flips. But on the outside, I just said, 'Now, son, you didn't get in until late. You need your rest. You've got to go to school tomorrow.'"

"No," he said, "I want to go."

She said, "I just acted like I didn't care if he went to church with me or not. But he did go to church with me."

Then she said, "The next Saturday night, the same thing happened. He got in about four o'clock.

But the next morning he got up and ate breakfast with me. Then he said, 'Mom, I believe I'll go to Sunday school and church with you this morning.'"

I told him, "But, son, you need your rest. You've got to go to school tomorrow."

"No," he said, "I want to go." So he went.

"Then that same Sunday night, he said, 'I believe I'll go to church with you tonight.' He went to church that night, and when the altar call was given, he went to the altar and got saved."

She said, "You know, before he was saved, he was one-hundred percent for the devil. But now that he's born again, he's one-hundred and twenty percent for God! I believe he's going to turn into a preacher!"

She added, "I'm so glad I've got a brand-new boy! I'm so glad you told me the things you did." Then she thanked me and turned around and walked off.

Then she came back and said, "Do you know what else? Not only have I got a brand-new boy, but he's got a brand-new mamma."

She said, "You know, I don't worry about him anymore. I learned how to pray in faith and walk in love.

"Sometimes I almost have to pinch myself and say, 'Is this really you?' because I think so differently now."

It makes a lot of difference, friends, when you walk in love. When you walk in love, your faith will work.

Sometimes people think they are believing God when really their faith is being hindered by lack of love.

And let me just say this while I'm at it. You can hinder your children from walking with God by raising them in a home where there is no love.

Children ought to have a right to be brought up in an atmosphere where the God-kind of love prevails in the home. They not only need to see your faith in demonstration, they need to see your love in demonstration. Then they'll go out in life and win!

My wife and I maintained that kind of atmosphere in our home. That's the reason we never had any problems with our children.

I don't mean they weren't children. Of course they were children and acted like children. But we believed the best about them, and we spoke the best about them.

When you see the worst in your children and are always telling them about it, they'll never amount to anything. They'll live up to what you say.

Children are going to miss it sometimes because they are children; you can't put a grown head on a child. But when you see the best in them and love them, you'll bring the best out of them, and they'll want to amount to something in life. They will live up to the God-kind of love that you instill in them.

The God-Kind of Love Fulfills the Law

Let's look at another Scripture in the Book of Galatians. Paul was writing to the churches in Galatia. These were Gentile churches, but this letter was not written to just one church.

It was written to be read by the churches throughout Galatia, and it applies to all Christians everywhere.

GALATIANS 5:14
14 For ALL THE LAW IS FULFILLED IN ONE WORD, even in this; THOU SHALT LOVE THY NEIGHBOUR AS THYSELF.

This Scripture says that all the Law is fulfilled in one word — love! It is fulfilled when we simply love our neighbors as ourselves. How much of the Law is fulfilled by walking in love? All of it!

When you're walking in the God-kind of love, you don't have to worry that you haven't obeyed some part of the Law, do you? When you are fulfilling the law of love, you don't have to be concerned about fulfilling a bunch of rules, regulations, and laws.

Some people fight small wars over whether or not we are to obey the Ten Commandments. Actually, it's so simple. The law of love includes the Ten Commandments. People stumble over the simplicity of what the Bible is telling us, and they miss the truth of the Word.

Sons of God Are Sons of Love

Notice something John said in the First Epistle of John. It tells us something more about the God-kind of love. The sons of God — God's born-again new creation — are to walk in the God-kind of love.

> 1 JOHN 3:1,2
> 1 Behold, what manner of love the Father hath bestowed upon us, that WE SHOULD BE CALLED THE SONS OF GOD: therefore the world knoweth us not, because it knew him not.
> 2 Beloved, NOW ARE WE THE SONS OF GOD. . . .

We are not just *going to be* the sons of God when we all get to Heaven in the sweet by and by. If we've been born again, we are the sons of God now. If we are sons of God, then we are sons of love because God is love, and we are made in His image.

Since God is love, and we are children of God, then we are children of love. When we were born again, the life of God was imparted into our spirits.

Believers are to let the life and the love of God dominate their being.

That is the reason we have to do something with our minds and bodies because divine love has not been shed abroad in our minds and bodies. And unless we do something about our fleshly nature, it will hinder us from walking in love.

Our unrenewed mind and our unregenerated flesh will try to dominate the inward man — the spirit man on the inside.

ROMANS 12:1,2
1 I beseech you therefore, brethren, by the mercies of God, that YE PRESENT YOUR BODIES A LIVING SACRIFICE, holy, acceptable unto God, which is your reasonable service.
2 And be not conformed to this world: but BE YE TRANSFORMED [How?] BY THE RENEWING OF YOUR MIND, that ye may prove what is that good, and acceptable, and perfect, will of God.

We need to get our minds renewed with the love of God! The Body of Christ hasn't really renewed their minds to the God-kind of love as we should have. But the Bible has much to say about renewing the mind. We will have to renew our minds if we're going to walk in love toward others.

You see, so many times, instead of accepting our responsibility as Christians, we want God to do all the work in our spiritual growth and development. We expect Him to supply more of something that He has already provided, when really it's our responsibility to see to it that we develop our love so it can grow and increase.

On the subject of the God-kind of love, too many believers are like the man with the one talent. He wrapped up his talent in a napkin and hid it. So many of us have hidden the love of God that has already been shed abroad in our hearts. We've hidden it, instead of using it, exercising it, and developing it.

No, we need to find out what God's Word says on the subject of love and renew our mind to what His Word says. Then we need to practice, exercise, and develop what God has already given us.

We need to be so saturated in God's Word that we will be saturated in His love. Then acting on the God-kind of love will be the first thought that comes into our mind, no matter what anyone has done to us.

The God-kind of love always asks the question, "How is what I'm about to do or say going to affect the other person?"

God will require us to walk in love even when others around us aren't walking in love toward us. We will have many occasions in life to exercise the love of God when others don't walk in love toward us.

I've had many such opportunities in my ministry. For example, on one occasion God spoke strongly to my heart about pastoring a certain church. The congregation wanted me to be their next pastor. But the former pastor wanted his cousin to pastor the church, so he began politicking in the church to get him elected instead.

The God-kind of love has never divided a church. I could have taken at least half of those church members and started another church because many of those people wanted me to be their next pastor. But I couldn't divide a church and walk in love, and no one else can either.

What astounds me is that some born-again, Spirit-filled Christians can be sheep thieves, divide churches, and steal another man's congregation, and it doesn't bother them in the least bit. Then they blame it on God, saying, "God told me to do it."

But God isn't that way! Either they lied or God lied about it because God said, "Love worketh no ill to his neighbour."

Anyway, I could have divided that church and started my own church with half of this former pastor's congregation. But I chose to listen to the inward man instead of to my flesh.

I listened to the love of God in me, and the Holy Spirit said to me, "You just go your way and don't divide this church." So even though I knew God had spoken to me about pastoring that church, I withdrew my name from the pastoral candidates and left town.

Later on, I said to the Lord, "Lord, what about that church? What's going to happen to those people?"

The Lord answered me by saying, "They will suffer because they aren't in My perfect will. They listened to the wrong people and put the wrong person in as pastor. But I'll take care of you because you acted in love."

Thank God, God did take care of me and in grand style too! And do you know that before a year had come and gone, God had installed me as the pastor of that church, and I didn't have a thing in the world to do with it either. God arranged it all!

Sometimes people's problem is that when God speaks to them, they try to run over other people to try to make what God told them come to pass. Then they get out of love, and God can't bless them because they aren't in a position spiritually to receive His blessings.

God wants to bless us all He can, of course. But He can't when we are not walking in His plan. You see, God's plan is that we walk in love toward others. I don't know about you, but I decided a long time ago that I'm going to walk in love whether anyone else does or not!

In the ministry, you'll have many opportunities to walk in love instead of in the flesh! For instance, every Pentecostal church I ever pastored, I had to pastor by walking in love because each one of them had the reputation for being a troubled church.

But in every situation, God taught me how to solve many of the problems in those churches just by walking in love and teaching the people about the God-kind of love. And God taught me how to love the sheep, not beat them.

One church in particular had a lot of problems. The church had been in existence twenty-three years, and I was just twenty-one years old when I took the pastorate.

In twenty-three years, many of those families had grown up and intermarried into other families in the church. Therefore, the church was made up of many people who were related to each other by marriage, and they were constantly getting into family squabbles. In order to pastor that church, I had to learn how to crucify the flesh and keep the body under.

There were some Sunday mornings in particular when it was all I could do to keep my flesh under. Sometimes I just felt like getting up in the pulpit and skinning them all alive and nailing their hides to the wall. I wanted to start with the deacon board first, and then take every Sunday school teacher one by one, and after I'd skinned them, I wanted to start skinning the entire congregation!

You talk about crucifying the flesh and keeping the flesh under subjection to my spirit! I had to learn how to do it in that church.

But instead of giving in to my flesh and skinning everyone alive, I just preached one Sunday on love and the next Sunday I'd preach on Heaven. Instead of giving in to my flesh and beating everyone over the head with the Word of God, I'd preach from First Corinthians 13, the love chapter.

If you can get everyone loving one another and everyone excited about their eternal hope in Heaven, many circumstances in the natural will just straighten themselves out.

People may squabble in the natural and get themselves into trouble, but they really want to rise to the level of spirituality God desires for them. And it will help them to rise to their full potential if you will tell them how God sees them instead of how the devil sees them. God's love working in and through us never fails.

Owe Nothing But Love

In the last part of Romans 13:8, we saw that love fulfills the Ten Commandments. But now let's look at the first part of this verse.

ROMANS 13:8
8   OWE NO MAN ANY THING, BUT TO LOVE ONE ANOTHER: for he that loveth another hath fulfilled the law.

Sometimes people take this verse out of its setting and make it say something it isn't saying. Many people have suffered as a result of doing that.

For example, some people use this verse to say we can't buy on credit.

Now we shouldn't go into debt so we can't pay our bills. But this verse doesn't mean we can't buy on credit. You ought to pay your bills, of course. And if you don't know how to use credit properly, you'll always get into debt, so you may have to give up buying on credit.

However, some people teach as doctrine that we aren't supposed to buy on credit. But think about it. You operate on credit every day. All of us do. Do you have electricity in your house? Don't you owe your electricity bill once a month? Do you use gas or water? You owe those bills, don't you?

If you're renting a house, you owe that bill. What would be the difference between owing a rental payment and owing a house payment? The only difference is that if you're making house payments, the house would eventually belong to you.

But if a person has good sense and uses it wisely, there is nothing wrong with buying on credit. Actually, even when you buy on credit, you don't owe it until the bill comes due. Then if you pay your bill on time, you still don't owe it because you paid it.

Some people can do the most foolish things, thinking they're obeying the Scriptures, when they're not listening to the Bible at all.

You see, you can't lift a part of a verse out of its setting and try to prove something with it. By doing so, as I sometimes humorously point out, you could prove you ought to go hang yourself.

One Scripture says, "Judas went out and hanged himself" (Matt. 27:5). Then you could go over to the verses about the Good Samaritan where Jesus said, "Go thou and do likewise" (Luke 10:37).

Well, if we put them together, we could say that Judas went out and hanged himself, so go thou and do likewise!

We may laugh at that and think it's funny, but it isn't any more funny than taking part of this verse in Romans 13:8 out of its setting to make it say something it isn't saying.

I heard about a minister once who did exactly that. In this minister's town, a certain Baptist church outgrew their facilities. The Baptist pastor decided to sell the building, but he wanted to sell it to believers so it could still be used for a church.

This other minister, who was also a pastor living in the same city, wanted to buy it. The Baptist pastor who was selling the church approached this minister, and said, "People who are now in Heaven have put money into this church so it could be a place for soulwinning.

"Now you folks believe in getting people saved, so we'd like to offer it to you." The Baptist pastor offered to sell the building to that other church at a ridiculously low price because he wanted the building to be used as a church.

Then one of the women in the Baptist church told her husband about it. He was a lawyer, and he wasn't saved, but he did come to church with his wife sometimes.

He told the minister who was interested in buying the church building, "If you want to buy that building, I'll furnish the money and loan it to you at two-percent interest. I don't want to make anything on it. But it would cost about that much for my secretary to take care of the paper work. Then after a year, I'll reduce it to one-percent interest."

This second minister said, "No, we can't buy the church building. I know you're selling it at an exceptionally low price. But the Bible says, 'Owe no man anything,' so we can't go into debt." And he passed up that business deal.

When I heard about that, I thought to myself, "Here they are making monthly lease payments for the building they're in now, and that doesn't even allow them to own anything. What's the difference if they make lease payments or mortgage payments! At least if they bought the property, they would own the building and could do what they wanted to with it!"

Do you know that within eighteen months there were only about thirty people left in that second minister's church! Finally, they just had to close down, and the minister left town.

You see, that's not what that Scripture means. It's dangerous to take a Scripture out of context and build a doctrine on it.

Another pastor and his wife started a church in their home, and they outgrew that and rented another facility.

They kept saving up money in their church building fund until they had $1.5 million in that account.

They used that money as a down payment on the facility, and then they renovated the building. After about two years, they had paid $4 million for the facility, but they owned it free and clear.

What if they hadn't taken that step of faith and put the $1.4 million as a down payment on the building?

You see, God blessed them because they put their hand to something. Now that congregation numbers more than 3,500 members.

The Scripture "Owe no man anything but love" does not apply to buying on credit. It has no reference to that situation whatsoever. But it does mean that we are not to get into bondage to people.

And it also means that we owe a debt of love to everyone, and that debt will never be paid off. We'll just have to keep on walking in love. *Weymouth's* translation of Roman 13:8 reads, "Leave no debt unpaid except the standing debt of mutual love."

The Bible says God will bless whatever we put our hand to (Deut. 28:12). If we don't put our hand to do something for the Lord, He doesn't have anything to bless. Some folks want to be blessed, but they're going to have to step out in faith and do something in order to get blessed.

God could bless these folks who stepped out in faith because they acted in faith. They set their hand to do something for the Lord. Therefore, God had something to work with so He could bless them.

The first church I mentioned didn't get blessed. They drew back from the blessing of the Lord, so they couldn't prosper. Within two years that church was closed. There wasn't a person in it, because the pastor didn't obey God's leading.

You see, if you left Tulsa on an airplane, and the pilot was off course just a little bit, by the time you were supposed to get to your destination, you'd be off course a lot.

But when you first started out, you weren't off course that much. However, if you don't correct yourself, in the process of time, you'd get off track a lot.

Spiritually speaking, it's the same way. If you get off course a little bit and you don't correct yourself, the further you go, the further away you'll get in your thinking from what the Word really says. Finally, it will give the devil access to your thinking, and it can just mess everything up.

I know another minister in years gone by who was a traveling evangelist. He bought a piece of property at a ridiculously low price. He had enough money on hand to pay cash for it. Then he converted the building into offices, because it wasn't originally used for offices.

But in the course of time, he outgrew that building. He wanted to buy some more land so he could build larger facilities.

Someone came along and offered him about three times as much money as he'd originally paid for the property. He had paid about $125,000 for the land, but he was offered $600,000 for the land and the building he'd remodeled. It doesn't sound big now, but back then that was a lot of money.

Now this minister could have taken that $600,000 and bought a larger piece of property, and he could have built on that. At least he would have owned the property. Then he could have made payments on the building that he had to construct.

But with the $600,000 profit he made on selling his property with the building on it, he decided not to buy more land. He said, "The Bible says, 'Owe no man anything,' and we'd have to pay for the building construction on a new piece of property, so we can't do it." Therefore, he didn't buy the property.

Instead, he took that $600,000 profit and went out and rented the whole floor of an office building. Then he tried to raise money so he could pay cash for the new property he wanted to buy. But in the meantime, he outgrew those office facilities, so he also had to rent the second floor of this office building too.

Well, he used up the $600,000 profit he'd made on the sale of his property on rental payments and had nothing to show for it! In fact, over a period of several years, he paid out $800,000 for rent!

He could have taken that $600,000 he got for the land, paid for a larger piece of property, and borrowed what he needed for construction. It probably wouldn't have been any more than his rental payments were, and at least he would have had a building that he owned.

But he took this Scripture, "Owe no man anything but love," out of context and decided, "We can't build an office building because we can't go into debt."

When the Bible says, "Owe no man anything but love," it means that love is a debt we owe everyone, and we will never get that debt paid.

Our long-term debt to everyone will be love. And we'll be paying on that debt as long as we live.

We'll have to keep on walking in love to pay off that debt! So let's get started! Let's learn to walk in the royal law of God's love so we can reap the benefits!

CONFESSION:

The love of God, the God-kind of love, has been shed abroad in my heart by the Holy Ghost. Therefore, I am a lover, even as my Heavenly Father is a Lover. I am not a hater.

Therefore, I will let that love — the love nature of God — dominate my entire being.

I will walk in the royal law of God. I will talk the God-kind of love. I will act in the God-kind of love, for I am a new creation in Christ Jesus.

Under the New Covenant, I'm going to walk in God's statutes and commandments by walking in the law of the New Covenant, which is to walk in the royal law of love.

Chapter 4
The God-Kind of Love Forgives

One characteristic of the God-kind of love is that it forgives. When God's love is in demonstration, there is an attitude of forgiveness because love and forgiveness go hand in hand.

You see, the God-kind of love has to be practiced or exercised before it will benefit you. One way you exercise God's love is to forgive. Love exercised can grow and develop.

In other words, when love is practiced, then it brings results. And love practiced not only brings results, it brings great rewards, not only in this life, but also in the life to come.

Now I want you to see something that Paul wrote to the Church at Ephesus about exercising the God-kind of love. It applies to every believer. I like to say it this way. The Holy Ghost spoke this spiritual truth through the Apostle Paul to believers everywhere.

> **EPHESIANS 4:32**
> **32 And be ye kind one to another, tenderhearted, FORGIVING ONE ANOTHER, even as God for Christ's sake hath forgiven you.**

What is the God-kind of love like? If you ask what the love of God is like, you are asking what God is like because God *is* love. The God-kind of love is full of kindness and is tenderhearted. Since God's love is kind and tenderhearted, it is always ready to forgive.

The Bible commands us to be kind to one another. This verse is addressed to Christians. Isn't it strange that the Holy Ghost would have to tell born-again people to be kind to each other? But He knew folks were just as human then as they are now.

So many times believers let their flesh and their unrenewed minds *dominate* them, instead of letting the love of God *constrain* them.

Sometimes I think people interpret this verse by saying that we are to forgive people only when they are kind to us. If they are kind and tenderhearted to us, then we're supposed to be kind and tenderhearted to them.

They interpret this verse that if people have done us wrong and talked about us, then it's all right for us to be hardhearted about it and get even by talking about them. But that's not what the Bible says.

And this Scripture doesn't say, "Forgive one another when the offense doesn't amount to too much. But if people have done a lot against you, then it's all right not to forgive them." It doesn't read that way, does it? But too many times that is the way people *practice* that verse.

Sanctification

God knew we needed to be told to be kind to one another because we live in bodies that have not yet been redeemed. The man on the inside gets born again, but the fellow on the outside is the same as he always was. The flesh doesn't want to be kind, tenderhearted, or forgiving. But, thank God, we will have new bodies when we get to Heaven.

1 CORINTHIANS 9:27
27 But I keep under my body, and bring it into subjection: lest that by any means, when I have preached to others, I myself should be a castaway.

Even though Paul was a new creation, he had to bring his body into subjection to the inward man. Bringing our bodies into subjection to our spirits is part of walking in sanctification before God.

Most people think this verse just refers to sexual sins. Well, it does refer to that all right, but there are also a lot of other ways that you've got to bring your flesh into subjection to your spirit.

It also applies in this area of sanctification. Your flesh doesn't want to be kind to other folks, especially if they don't treat you exactly as you think they ought to. Your flesh wants to shun them and get back at them.

But you've got to keep the flesh under, because if you don't, you're going to run into trouble. If your flesh dominates you, you won't be able to walk in the God-kind of love. If you don't walk in love, then your faith won't work.

Learning how to walk in love and keep the flesh under is where sanctification comes in. Until you're raptured, you will continue to have that old, unredeemed nature in your flesh to deal with because your flesh didn't get converted.

God is not going to do anything with your body while you are on this earth; He already did something with your spirit. Now it's up to *you* to do something with your body and your mind. That's your responsibility as a Christian.

You see, sanctification isn't an experience you receive once and for all and that's the end of it. Sanctification is an ongoing lifestyle of keeping your flesh under control for the rest of your life. It involves a lifestyle of renewing your mind and walking in the God-kind of love.

Too many Christians allow their flesh to dominate and rule them. Then they wonder why they aren't receiving God's best in their lives. But it's impossible to walk in the God-kind of love if you're going to allow the flesh to rule you.

So if we're going to obey the Bible, we will have to let the inward man dominate us so we can be "kind one to another, tenderhearted, forgiving one another."

The inward man has those qualities because of the love of God. But we will have to practice forgiving one another even as God for Christ's sake forgave us.

As Christians, we have to "put on" Christ concerning the outward man. That doesn't happen automatically.

ROMANS 13:14
**14 But put ye on the Lord Jesus Christ, and make
not provision for the flesh, to fulfil the lusts
thereof.**

It's only as we "put on" Christ and make no provision for the flesh that we will be able to forgive one another even as God for Christ's sake forgave us.

The God-Kind of Love Forgives and Forgets

How can we forgive like God forgives? Well, the Bible says that God is love. And the same kind of love that God *is* has been shed abroad in our hearts or spirits in our inner man by the Holy Spirit.

What kind of love is it? Is it natural, human love? No, it is divine love. It is the God-kind of love. And one characteristic of the God-kind of love is that it forgives.

Let's look in the Word and see how God forgives. One thing about divine love — when God forgives, He forgets!

Once we repent and ask God's forgiveness, He blots out our transgressions and doesn't remember our sins anymore.

ISAIAH 43:25
**25 I, even I, am he that BLOTTETH OUT THY
TRANSGRESSIONS for mine own sake, and WILL
NOT REMEMBER thy sins.**

Under the New Covenant, God again tells us how He forgives.

HEBREWS 8:12
**12 For I will be merciful to their unrighteousness,
and THEIR SINS AND THEIR INIQUITIES WILL I
REMEMBER NO MORE.**

How does God forgive? These Scriptures tell us that
once we ask forgiveness, God doesn't remember our sins
anymore. No more! This verse doesn't say, "I'm going to
hold everything you've ever done against you, and I'm
going to remind you of your sins every time I think of
them."

Can you imagine that! What if every time we prayed,
God reminded us of everything we'd ever done in the
past? We wouldn't have any faith, would we? We'd constantly be feeling guilty about our past. We wouldn't
come boldly before Him and expect to receive anything
from Him because we'd constantly be feeling condemned.

Aren't you glad God forgives and forgets! Thank God,
this verse said that when we ask forgiveness, God will
remember our sins *no more!* The Bible says He is faithful and just to forgive us (1 John 1:9).

Sometimes husbands and wives can be prone to
remind each other of their past mistakes every time
something happens. There's no way they can develop a
good relationship if they keep doing that. Not only that,
but constantly reminding each other of past mistakes
and failures will ruin their prayer lives, and it will make
their faith inoperative.

1 PETER 3:7
**7   Likewise, ye husbands, dwell with them
according to knowledge, giving honour unto the**

wife, as unto the weaker vessel, and as being heirs together of the grace of life; THAT YOUR PRAYERS BE NOT HINDERED.

This verse is telling us what hinders prayers. God wants us to have unhindered prayers. If husbands and wives hold unforgiveness and ill will against each other, it can affect their health, and their prayers will be hindered. Their faith won't work.

Husbands and wives need to forgive like God forgives. They should be able to say to one another, "Honey, forgive me. I was wrong. I was short with you."

Unforgiveness and ill will is going to affect your prayer life! Love and forgiveness and faith all work together. In fact, you can't separate one of them from the other.

You want your prayers to be *un*hindered, don't you? Then walk in love and forgiveness because according to this verse, you can hinder your own prayers. Learn to forgive and forget like God does.

I was holding a meeting for a certain minister in the '30s, and then later I preached for his brother too. Both of them were Full Gospel pastors. The older brother had a much better personality than the younger one, and he was just a better preacher in every respect. Actually, he could just preach circles around the younger brother.

Even though the younger brother didn't have near the personality of the older brother, and he wasn't as good a preacher, he always pastored a good church and drove a new automobile even in Depression Days. In fact, he had a much larger church than the older brother. The older brother never was very successful in the ministry even though he had a better personality and was a better preacher.

Someone said to me, "I've got it figured out why the older brother never was very successful pastoring. Before he got saved, he was always meaner than the other brother. He was wicked, so now he's just paying for his sins. God is just punishing him."

I said to him, "How could God punish him when the Lord doesn't even remember that the man did anything wrong?"

How in the world is God going to punish you for something He doesn't even remember you did? God washes away and forgets your past when you are born again; you become a *new* creature.

No, I found out why one of them was a success in the ministry and the other one wasn't. The older brother with the better personality had all the ability, all right. He had tremendous speaking ability, and he could preach circles around his younger brother, but he never studied.

My wife and I stayed at the parsonage with the older brother, and he was always out talking to people and telling jokes. They weren't bad jokes, but it's just that telling jokes took up all his time. Then once he got in the pulpit, he didn't have anything to talk about but jokes. Once in awhile he'd get down to business and really preach.

But the other fellow was constantly studying. I know because I held a meeting for him. I mean he'd be in his study every day for several hours just pouring over the Bible and his books. You never did see him because he was busy studying.

And then at other times I stopped by to visit him, and he was always in his study with his Bible and his books just studying. That's why he climbed to the top in the ministry.

It wasn't a matter that one of them was being punished for his past, because when God forgives, He *forgets*! And that is the way He wants you and me to forgive too. If you walk in the God-kind of love, that is the way you will forgive, too, because *love and forgiveness go hand in hand*.

God Looks on the Heart

I was holding a meeting in a certain church, and it just seemed like we were struggling in the services. We'd been going for about a week and a half, and it seemed like nothing was happening.

But one night the Holy Ghost moved in a remarkable way. There was a person in the congregation whom the Holy Ghost used in gifts of the Spirit in a dynamic, supernatural way, and as a result, very outstanding things happened.

As I stood there on the platform, I said to myself, *This is the turning point of these meetings.* And it was. That meeting just changed all the rest of the services. It was marvelous.

But I went home, and I couldn't go to sleep. And I'll tell you why I couldn't sleep. A day or two before this meeting, I'd been driving down a street in this large city, and I saw this person who'd been so marvelously used in the meeting. I saw him walking down the street, and I saw him go into a certain place that was just a dark dive.

That night when I couldn't sleep, I kept seeing that man go into that place, and that just kept working in the back of my mind. Finally, I just couldn't get it off my mind.

So about 12:30 in the night, I just sat bolt upright in the bed and said, "All right, Lord, all right. Let's just have it out. Now how come You used that fellow? I saw that fellow go into that dark dive. How could You use *him?*"

I continued: "You know that there are some holy saints of God in that church who have been living right for fifty or sixty years. Why couldn't You have used them instead?"

Just like someone was standing in the room, the Lord answered, "Well, you see, you go by sight. You saw that fellow go in that place, all right. But then you went on down the street, and what you didn't see was that he got inside that place and suddenly came to himself and said, 'What in the world am I doing in here? Dear God, forgive me.' And he turned around and walked out of there."

Then the Lord said, "Besides that, he asked Me to forgive him, so I didn't even remember that he'd ever done anything wrong. Therefore, I could use him just as much as I could use a person who had been living right for sixty years."

That taught me something. When God *forgives*, He *forgets*. God said, *"I, even I, am he that blotteth out thy transgressions for mine own sake, and WILL NOT REMEMBER THY SINS"* (Isa. 43:25).

So if God can forget about your mistakes and your past, you need to forget about them too! Then you need to forgive and forget about other people's past mistakes too.

Forgive people just like God forgives you so you can stay in the love walk. Let the love of God dominate you. Then you can claim the victory in every area of your life.

You see, if you really love people and forgive them, you will not keep reminding them of their past mistakes, sins, and failures. You will not keep reminding them about the way they hurt you, let you down, or offended you.

Now the devil may bring a picture to your mind of something that happened between you and another person. But you don't have to entertain the devil's thoughts.

If you were in the wrong, and you've repented and confessed it to God, God has forgiven you.

If the devil brings a picture reminding you what someone else did to you, just laugh at Satan and say, "Mr. Devil, that happened all right. But that is just a picture of what happened because I've forgiven that person. As far as I am concerned, that doesn't exist any-more."

Then go on your way and walk in forgiveness, know-ing that the Lord has forgiven you.

Forgiveness Under the New Covenant

Under the New Covenant, how are we to forgive? As people forgive us? No, we forgive like Ephesians 4:32 says: ". . . *be ye kind one to another, tenderhearted, FORGIVING ONE ANOTHER, EVEN AS GOD for Christ's sake HATH FORGIVEN YOU.*"

We forgive as God for Christ's sake has forgiven us. We forgive even as God forgives. In other words, we for-give whether people forgive us or not.

How does God forgive us? Well, God is love. God said, "I will not remember your iniquities" (Heb. 10:17). Therefore, *love* says, "I will not remember your iniqui-ties."

If God forgives us and does not remember our iniq-uities because He loves us, then we need to forgive one another and not remember their sins either. Forgive-ness is part of walking in the New Covenant law of love.

Some people say, "Well, *I* just can't forgive." But that doesn't line up with the Scriptures, because if you are born again, the God-kind of love has been shed abroad in your heart.

Other people say, "Well, I can't forgive the way God does because I'm not God." Of course you're not God.

But, you see, God forgives because He is love (1 John 4:8). And the same kind of love that God *is* dwells in you. Therefore, you *can* forgive with His love, just as God does.

Because the love of God has been shed abroad in our hearts by the Holy Ghost, that means that God even furnishes the love for you and me to forgive with. But too many believers make the mistake of going by their head instead of their heart.

Aren't you glad God said, "I'll not remember your iniquities" (Isa. 43:25; Ps. 103:3)! In another Scripture, He said, "He will cast all our sins into the depths of the sea" (Micah 7:19).

Isn't that wonderful! If we've repented and asked God's forgiveness, God doesn't remember that you or I ever did anything wrong.

You ask, "How can He do that?" Because the Bible says that love *covers* or *blots out* a multitude of sins (1 Peter 4:8).

So divine love not only forgives, it forgets! That's the way God wants us to forgive too. And we can forgive and forget because God has already furnished His love in our hearts so we can forgive. Therefore, there's no excuse for failure in our ability to forgive.

Forgiveness Doesn't Hold On to Grudges

If you say you have forgiven someone, but you hold on to grudges in your heart, then you haven't really forgiven at all.

COLOSSIANS 3:13
**13 Forbearing one another, and FORGIVING ONE
ANOTHER, IF ANY MAN HAVE A QUARREL
AGAINST ANY: EVEN AS CHRIST FORGAVE YOU,
so also do ye.**

In 1939 my wife and I went to pastor a church in
north Texas. The first week we were there, one of the
women in the church came to visit us.

We talked for a while, and then she said, "Brother
Hagin, I want to tell you about Sister So-and-so and
how she treated me." Then she began to go on and on
telling us how that sister had mistreated her.

I thought to myself, *Well, last week she and this
other sister probably got into a spat.* I asked her, "When
did this happen?"

She began to count, "One, two, three, four, five, six,
seven, eight. . ." I thought she was going to say, "Eight
days ago." But she answered, "It will be eight years ago
next Tuesday."

I had such a look of astonishment on my face that
she quickly answered, "Now don't misunderstand me.
I've forgiven her all right. But I never will forget how
that old devil treated me."

Without thinking, I answered, "Sister, you're a bald-
faced liar. You haven't forgiven her. If you had forgiven
her, you would have forgotten it, and you wouldn't be
over here telling me about it."

You see, when we walk in the light of the Word,
then we can enjoy all the benefits thereof. But to walk

in the light of the Word, you'll have to walk in love and forgiveness.

The Bible said, *"And above all things have fervent charity among yourselves: for charity shall cover the multitude of sins"* (1 Peter 4:8). This sister said she had forgiven the other woman, but she wasn't walking in the light of what the Word says about love and forgiveness. If she had, she would have covered it over with love and forgotten about it.

Unforgiveness: A Hindrance to Faith and Prayer

There is something else we need to see about how love and forgiveness work together. Unforgiveness — the lack of forgiveness — is one hindrance to *prayer* that Jesus mentioned.

> **MARK 11:23-25**
> **23 For verily I say unto you, That whosoever shall say unto this mountain, Be thou removed, and be thou cast into the sea; and shall not doubt in his heart, but shall believe that those things which he saith shall come to pass; he shall have whatsoever he saith.**
> **24 Therefore I say unto you, What things soever ye desire, when ye pray, believe that ye receive them, and ye shall have them.**
> **25 And when ye stand PRAYING, FORGIVE, if ye have ought against any: that your Father also which is in heaven may forgive you your trespasses.**

A lot of times people take these verses out of context and make them say something they don't say and try to make them work. But, you see, there are some conditions involved in getting Mark 11:23 and 24 to work. Did you ever notice that many of the promises of God are conditional?

You see, the blessings of God don't just fall on us like ripe cherries off a tree. You have your part to play — your responsibility in the matter.

When Jesus tells us in Mark 11:23,24 that we can have what we say, we all rejoice and are thrilled with those truths. And we should be. But do you know that is not all Jesus said about answered prayer?

Mark 11:23 and 24 do not present the whole story on the subject of faith. For example, in Galatians 5:6, the Bible has something else to say about faith. It says that faith only works by love.

GALATIANS 5:6
6   For in Jesus Christ neither circumcision availeth any thing, nor uncircumcision; BUT FAITH WHICH WORKETH BY LOVE.

So you won't be able to get your faith to work for you if you're not walking in love and forgiveness. I don't care how many biblical confessions you make or how scriptural they are — your faith won't work without the God-kind of love.

You can make all the confessions you want, but they won't work for you unless you forgive. You can get up every morning and go through your list, take time out at noon to speak faith confessions, and even get up in the middle of the night and repeat the same confessions — and your faith still won't work for you unless you're walking in love.

You can even quote your faith confessions like that for a hundred years, but your faith just will not work in an atmosphere of unforgiveness.

You see, believing you have your petition and confessing your faith with your mouth is only part of effective faith and receiving answers to prayer. In fact, Mark 11:23 and 24 won't work without Mark 11:25: *"And when ye stand PRAYING, forgive. . . ."* Why won't they work without Mark 11:25? Because faith won't work without love, and love forgives.

Notice that verse 25 begins with the word "and." The word "and" is a conjunction. It joins what Jesus just finished saying to what He's about to say.

Notice what Jesus had just said in Mark 11:24: *"Therefore I say unto you, What things soever ye desire, when YE PRAY. . . ."* Jesus is talking about prayer. And He is talking about how to make your faith effectual.

In verse 25, Jesus said, "When ye stand praying, if ye have ought against any, forgive." When you pray — forgive.

Why did Jesus say that? Because Jesus knows that if we have an air of unforgiveness about us, our prayers wouldn't be effectual. Faith only works by love (Gal. 5:6). Love forgives because God is love, and God forgives.

Now if Jesus had just said, "When you stand praying, you'll have your petition," we'd all have it made.

But He didn't stop there. He said that when we stand praying, *we* have to do something. What do we have to do? Forgive! If we have ought against anyone, we have to forgive.

Prayer and faith won't work when there is an air of unforgiveness about you! And *unforgiveness* is what has so many people stymied in their faith and their prayer life.

Can you see that? Faith in your prayer life won't work unless you are a forgiving person. So when you stand praying, forgive. In fact, have you ever thought about it? Sometimes it takes faith just to forgive! But it will hinder your prayer life if you don't forgive.

We preach a lot about forgiveness and hear a lot about forgiving others, but some way or another, we just don't practice it the way the Bible said it. And when you really begin to study what the Bible has to say about forgiveness, and you really get into detail about the subject, it's almost shocking what God has to say about it.

For example, let's look at a parable Jesus gave the disciples. Peter had just asked Jesus how many times he had to forgive his brother. Jesus said, "Until seventy times seven" (Matt. 18:22). Then to illustrate that point, Jesus told His disciples this parable.

MATTHEW 18:23-35
23 Therefore is the kingdom of heaven likened unto a certain king, which would take account of his servants.

24 And when he had begun to reckon, one was brought unto him, which owed him ten thousand talents.

25 But forasmuch as he had not to pay, his lord commanded him to be sold, and his wife, and children, and all that he had, and payment to be made.

26 The servant therefore fell down, and worshipped him, saying, Lord, have patience with me, and I will pay thee all.

27 Then the lord of that servant was moved with compassion, and loosed him, and FORGAVE HIM THE DEBT.

28 But the same servant went out, and found one of his fellowservants, which owed him an hundred pence: and he laid hands on him, and took him by the throat, saying, Pay me that thou owest.

29 And his fellowservant fell down at his feet, and besought him, saying, Have patience with me, and I will pay thee all.

30 And he would not: but went and cast him into prison, till he should pay the debt.

31 So when his fellowservants saw what was done, they were very sorry, and came and told unto their lord all that was done.

32 Then his lord, after that he had called him, said unto him, O THOU WICKED SERVANT, I FORGAVE THEE ALL THAT DEBT, because thou desiredst me:

33 SHOULDEST NOT THOU ALSO HAVE HAD COMPASSION ON THY FELLOWSERVANT, even as I had pity on thee?

34 And his lord was wroth, and delivered him to the tormentors, till he should pay all that was due unto him.

35 So likewise shall my heavenly Father do also unto you, IF YE FROM YOUR HEARTS FORGIVE

NOT EVERY ONE HIS BROTHER THEIR TRESPASSES.

Notice that his master called this servant "wicked." Why did he call him wicked? Just because he wasn't willing to forgive! Now there's no use in getting into a discussion on what's more wicked or less wicked. I mean, if it's wicked, we don't want to have anything to do with it. If it's wicked, it doesn't belong to us, and we don't have any business with it.

Also notice something else in this Scripture. Compassion and forgiveness go hand in hand. Verse 33 says, *"Shouldest not thou also have had compassion on thy fellowservant, even as I had pity on thee?"*

Whether you realize it or not, a lack of compassion and an unwillingness to forgive others are the things that hinder us from receiving from God and from growing spiritually. Unforgiveness will hinder us from being *what* God wants us to be and from being *who* God wants us to be.

God tells us exactly what He thinks about unforgiveness: *"So likewise shall my heavenly Father do also unto you, if ye from your hearts forgive not every one his brother their trespasses"* (v. 35).

Well, we don't want to be classed with this wicked servant, do we? Jesus called this servant wicked just because he refused to forgive. So from our hearts let's forgive every one who has done anything wrong to us!

I know from experience of more than fifty years of ministry and talking with many thousands of people through the years on a one-to-one basis, that unforgiveness is the main reason why people's faith doesn't work. And unforgiveness is the main reason why people fail to receive their healing.

In fact, go through the four Gospels and search the Scriptures for yourself, and write out every verse Jesus ever mentioned relative to faith.

You will find that unforgiveness — the lack of walking in love — is a specific hindrance to faith and prayer that Jesus mentioned (Mark 11:23-25). That doesn't mean there aren't other hindrances to faith and prayer. But what it does mean is that unforgiveness is the *main* hindrance to faith and answered prayer.

People have some of the fuzziest ideas about spiritual things you've ever seen, especially when it comes to love and forgiveness.

For example, most folks know it is wrong to hold some big grudge against someone. But they seem to think they can get by with it if it's just a *little* grudge or a *little* unforgiveness.

They think, *Well, just holding some little bitty grudge against someone won't hurt anything.*

But think about it. In Mark 11:25, Jesus said, "When you stand praying, forgive if ye have *ought* against anyone."

The word "ought" means any kind of grudge or ill will or wrong feeling about anyone at all. That means a little grudge, a middle-sized grudge, or a big grudge — *anything at all* against another person.

After all, the Bible says it's the little foxes that spoil the vine (Song of Sol. 2:15). So many times it's not the big things in believers' lives that spoil their Christian walk. It's the many little sins they fail to deal with that destroy their faith.

Sometimes it's the little sins you overlook that keep your faith from working and your prayers from being heard. Sometimes it's the little "oughts" — the little grudges against others — that you don't think amount to much that will keep your voice from being heard on High.

Be Quick To Repent and Quick To Believe

A woman once asked me a question along this line. She said, "Brother Hagin, there's no family in this church who has been as faithful as my family has been. Yet if one member of our family has ever received healing, I don't know it. But my husband's family is not nearly as faithful, yet they always receive their healing. Why is that?"

I said, "I don't know why one person gets healed and another one doesn't unless God reveals it to me. But I know this, if people get results over a long period of time, it's because they're walking in line with God's Word."

Then I said, "Without knowing your husband's family, I would say that if they always receive their healing, they have two outstanding characteristics.

First, they are quick to repent and forgive. You understand that repentance and forgiveness go hand in hand. And, second, they are quick to believe."

That woman's eyes got big, and her mouth fell open. She said, "Why, Brother Hagin, you've hit the nail right on the head!"

I answered, "No, I didn't hit the nail on the head. God did. I'm not that smart. I got the answer from Mark 11:23-25."

The Bible has the answer to every problem and to every situation in life. No matter what happens in life, the Bible has the answer. It may not be the answer we want to hear, but it's the answer.

She said, "I believe my husband's family are the quickest to repent and forgive of any people I've ever known."

This woman added, "Not only that, but if there was a squabble, they'd take all the responsibility for it, even when they weren't to blame.

"They would forgive you, no matter what you had done to them. They wouldn't hold anything against anyone, not even for a moment. They'd always say, 'I'm to blame. Please forgive me.' And they meant it."

Then she said, "My husband's family lived in the country, and it's hard for them to get to church. But when they would come to church, they'd go to the altar, repent the fastest and believe God the quickest, and get blessed the most of anyone I've ever seen in my life."

God just blesses people who repent, forgive, and believe.

Smith Wigglesworth once said, "There's just something about believing God that will cause God to pass over a million people just to get to you."

This woman continued, "But you take my family — we will eventually forgive because we know we have to, but we'll hold out just as long as we dare."

But, you see, the problem is that a person could die while he's holding out. Then she said, "And when it comes to believing, we're the slowest people you've ever seen to believe God."

She had her answer right there. People who are slow to repent and slow to forgive aren't going to be able to believe God for His best, because faith is of the heart.

If there is unforgiveness in their *heart*, it will hinder them from being able to believe God.

You see, love and forgiveness go hand in hand. Love forgives. Love worketh no ill to its neighbor. Therefore, love doesn't take account of a suffered wrong (1 Cor. 13:5 *Amp.*).

When you walk in love, you fulfill the Law — all of God's requirements. Without love, you won't be able to walk in God's ways because God *is* love.

Even though all the blessings of God have already been provided for you through Jesus Christ, there's no way you can have faith to receive the blessings of God in your life with unforgiveness in your heart. That's absolutely the truth!

It doesn't make any difference how spiritual you are or how many gifts of the Spirit operate through you, there are certain qualifications you have to meet if you're going to enjoy God's best in this life. Be quick to repent, quick to forgive, and quick to believe God.

Forgive Yourself Too!

You not only have to forgive others, you also have to forgive yourself! It's hard sometimes to forgive yourself for missing it and failing, isn't it? But you have to do it if you want your faith and prayers to work!

If you don't forgive yourself, it can keep you from receiving healing, and it can keep your prayers from being answered because your faith won't work except by love.

If you don't forgive yourself, it will hinder your faith just as much as unforgiveness toward another person will hinder your faith. It's just as wrong not to forgive *yourself* and to harbor ill will and animosity against yourself as it is not to forgive someone else.

> 1 JOHN 3:18-21
> 18 My little children, let us not love in word, neither in tongue; but in deed and in truth.
> 19 And hereby we know that we are of the truth, and shall assure our hearts before him.
> 20 FOR IF OUR HEART CONDEMN US, God is greater than our heart, and knoweth all things.
> 21 Beloved, IF OUR HEART CONDEMN US NOT, THEN HAVE WE CONFIDENCE TOWARD GOD.

You see, if you harbor unforgiveness and ill will in your heart, your heart will condemn you, and you won't be able to come boldly before God to get your petitions answered. Your prayers will be hindered.

But if you walk in love, your heart won't condemn you. If you'll forgive — not only others, but forgive *yourself* — your heart will not condemn you. Then you will have confidence in coming before God in prayer.

You know yourself that sometimes when you come into the Presence of God to pray, the devil will bring all kinds of accusations against you to try to keep you from praying. And invariably he will bring up your past to try to hinder you and keep you from receiving what you need from God.

When the devil accuses you of past failures, he's just bringing a photo into your mind — a picture — of your past, because if you've asked God to forgive you, your past sins don't exist anymore.

God said that He blotted out your sins. If God blotted them out, then they don't exist anymore.

ISAIAH 43:25,26
25 I, even I, AM HE THAT BLOTTETH OUT thy transgressions FOR MINE OWN SAKE, and WILL NOT REMEMBER THY SINS.
26 Put me in remembrance: let us plead together: declare thou, that thou mayest be justified.

I want you to notice something about these verses. In Isaiah 43:25, God is telling us that He blots out our sins. He is describing the God-kind of forgiveness. He not only blots *out* our sins, but then He also forgets them.

Then in verse 26, God says, *"Put me in remembrance: let us plead together. . . ."* In this verse, He's talking about prayer. The margin of my Bible says, "Set forth your case." That's an invitation from God to come before Him, setting forth your case in prayer so He can bless you.

But you won't be able to set forth your case in prayer to God unless you learn to forget your mistakes! If you haven't recognized the truth in verse 25, *"I, even I, am he that blotteth out thy transgressions,"* then you will be hindered from setting forth your cause and your case before God.

Unless you recognize that your sins have been blotted out, Satan will whip you in prayer by constantly bringing up past transgressions. But it's not enough just to recognize that your sins are forgiven and blotted out. Then you need to *forgive* yourself for the mistakes you've made and *forget* your past.

Otherwise, you may forgive others, all right, but you can condemn yourself. You will think such things as, "I'm such a failure. I've made such a mess of my life and such a fool of myself."

Remember something Saul said. He said, *"I have sinned. . . : behold, I have played the fool, and have erred exceedingly"* (1 Sam. 26:21). We have all sinned and missed it from time to time. But we have to forgive ourselves so we can go on and succeed in God. We won't be able to succeed at anything if our past is weighing us down.

And as long as you allow the devil to keep reminding you of past sins and failures, he will take advantage of you. Constantly dwelling on the past will keep your faith inoperative. And as long as you have no confidence in your own faith, your prayers will be hindered.

I want you to notice something else verse 25 says. Did God say He has blotted out our transgressions for *our* sakes? No, He said He's blotted out our sins ". . . *for MINE OWN sake. . . ."*

Why does God say that He won't remember our sins for His *own* sake? So that He can bless us! He blots out our sins for His own sake so He can help us and demonstrate His great mercy and love on our behalf. Of course, we are the ones who receive the benefit of God's forgiveness.

Once you recognize that your sins have been blotted out, then you can do what verse 26 says. You can pray effectively by bringing your case before God. But you can only do that when you learn to forget!

Some folks just need to go on record with God as having forgiven themselves. If you need to forgive others, do that too. But also forgive yourself for past mistakes, failures, and faults. Then forget about your mistakes. Love *forgets*. Unless you *forget* about your mistakes and failures, you really haven't forgiven yourself.

I was holding a meeting in a large city. I laid hands on a particular man several times. He was a businessman and a member of the church where I was holding the meeting. Practically every healing evangelist in America at that time had laid hands on this man, but he was still sick.

The Lord told me to talk to him, so I told the man to come early to the meeting the next night. I knew he had a heart condition.

The doctors had told him he might live two more years if he retired, stayed on medication, and spent most of his time resting. But he was only fifty-six years old. He didn't want to retire yet.

I was shaving and getting ready to go to church the next evening, when the Lord spoke to me. He said, "Do you think I would require you to do something I wouldn't be willing to do?"

I said, "No, Lord. You wouldn't do that because that would be unjust, and You're not unjust."

I finished shaving and was getting dressed, and the Lord spoke to me again and said the same thing. "Do you think I would require you to do something I wouldn't be willing to do?"

I said, "No. No, because if You required me to do something You wouldn't be willing to do, it would be unjust, and You're not unjust."

I finished getting ready and drove off to church. In the car the Lord said the same thing to me. I answered Him the same way. Then the Lord gave me these passages of Scripture in Matthew and Luke.

MATTHEW 18:21,22
21 Then came Peter to him, and said, Lord, how oft shall my brother sin against me, and I forgive him? till seven times?
22 Jesus saith unto him, I say not unto thee, Until seven times: but, UNTIL SEVENTY TIMES SEVEN.

LUKE 17:3-5
3   Take heed to yourselves: If thy brother trespass against thee, rebuke him; and if he repent, forgive him.

**4   And if he trespass against thee seven times IN
A DAY, and seven times IN A DAY turn again to
thee, saying, I repent; thou shalt forgive him.
5   And the apostles said unto the Lord,
INCREASE OUR FAITH.**

When Jesus said we were supposed to forgive seventy times seven, that doesn't mean in a lifetime —
that means in one day. That should tell us we are to
practice an attitude of forgiveness!

Also, notice that after Jesus talked about forgiveness, immediately the disciples said to Him, "Increase
our faith." Sometimes it takes faith to forgive people,
doesn't it? Also, you won't be able to increase your faith
until you forgive! That's absolutely the truth.

When the Lord gave me these Scriptures and said
this to me, I wondered why He was telling me this.

Then He said to me, "If I required you to forgive
your brother if he sinned against you 490 times in a
day, but I wasn't willing to do the same thing, then I
would be unjust."

I still didn't know why the Lord was saying this to
me, but I went on to church to talk to this man before
the service started. As soon as I started talking to him,
I understood exactly why the Lord said all this to me.

This man told me, "I have heart trouble and my kid-
neys are failing. The doctors told me that if I would sell
my business and lie around and rest and stay on medication, I might live a couple of years.

"But they said if I keep going the way I'm going, I
could just fall dead at any time."

Then this businessman told me, "I've been a member of a Full Gospel church for 35 years. Brother Hagin, I'll be honest with you. I know you teach faith, but every time I go forward to get healed, I know God won't heal me."

"Why won't He?" I asked.

"Well, I've just failed and missed it so many times. I've just sinned."

Even though I knew he had committed no sin too big for God to forgive, I asked, "What awful sin have you committed? Have you robbed a bank or killed someone?"

"No. No."

"Well, what awful sin have you ever committed?"

He said, "As far as I know, I haven't committed any awful sin. I've just searched my heart. But I own my own business, and I've made good money. I've always paid my tithes to my church and supported missions. But I could have given so much more financially than what I have given. I could have prayed so much more than I have. I've committed sins of omission."

Many believers get their mind just on sins of commission, but the Bible also teaches that there are sins of omission. Sins of omission are sins of failing to do right when it's in your power to do so. The Bible does say, ". . . *to him that knoweth to do good, and doeth it not, to him it is sin*" (James 4:17).

I began to tell this businessman what the Lord told me. I said, "Do you think the Lord would require you to do something He wouldn't be willing to do?"

"No, He wouldn't do that." And I began to show him
the Scriptures that the Lord gave me in Matthew and
Luke. Then I showed him James 5:14,15.

JAMES 5:14,15
14 Is any sick among you? let him call for the
elders of the church; and let them pray over him,
anointing him with oil in the name of the Lord:
15 And the prayer of faith shall save the sick, and
the Lord shall raise him up; AND IF HE HAVE
COMMITTED SINS, THEY SHALL BE FORGIVEN
HIM.

Did you notice that the Bible didn't say, "If he has
committed *a* sin" — *singular*. It said, "If he has committed *sins*" — *plural*. Then it says, "they *shall* be forgiven
him." It doesn't say that maybe his sins would be forgiven. It says they *shall* be forgiven!

I told him, "God is not only willing to heal you, He is
willing to forgive you, even for sins of omission. The
Lord has forgiven you, so quit accusing yourself. You
know what your problem is? You haven't forgiven yourself. Besides that, have you failed 490 times in one
day?"

"No," he said.

"Well then, you've got a good margin to operate on,"
I said.

Just as soon as this man forgave himself, his faith
started working. The unforgiveness that he'd held
against himself had hindered his faith. I laid hands on
him and prayed for him, and he was instantly healed.

Years later I was preaching in the same state, and one of this man's relatives told me about him. He said, "He ran his business all these years, and he finally sold his business and retired at seventy-five years of age."

According to medical science, He could easily have been dead at fifty-six because his heart was in such bad condition. Until he forgave himself for his past failures, he couldn't receive his healing.

You see, so many times believers can get tangled up in this sin business. What do I mean by that? I mean that some believers think one sin is really bad and another one isn't so bad. They think that God will excuse them for the little sins, but He can't forgive the big ones. If we're not careful, we can get all tangled up in our human thinking about sin.

But what does the Bible say about sin?

1 JOHN 2:1,2
1   My little children, these things write I unto you, that ye sin not. And IF ANY MAN SIN, WE HAVE AN ADVOCATE WITH THE FATHER, JESUS CHRIST THE RIGHTEOUS:
2   And HE IS THE PROPITIATION FOR OUR SINS: and not for ours only, but also for the sins of the whole world.

Jesus Christ the Righteous is the propitiation for *all* our sins — sins of commission as well as sins of omission. But to this man, this sin of omission was so bad that God couldn't forgive him for it. Maybe God could forgive him for other sins, but not this one. However, that's not what the Bible says.

JAMES 2:10,11
10 For WHOSOEVER SHALL KEEP THE WHOLE LAW, and YET OFFEND IN ONE POINT, HE IS GUILTY OF ALL.
11 For he that said, Do not commit adultery, said also, Do not kill. Now if thou commit no adultery, yet if thou kill, thou art become a transgressor of the law.

The Bible says if you keep the whole Law but offend in just one point, you are guilty in all points. What does that mean? It means if you commit one sin, you're just as guilty as if you commit another one. For example, if you bear false witness against your neighbor, you're just as guilty as the fellow who stole from his neighbor.

That doesn't line up with our human thinking, does it? But that's the reason the Word of God said, *"For all have sinned, and come short of the glory of God"* (Rom. 3:23).

Some people say, "Well, I'm not as bad as the other fellow." But you've got to remember that sin is sin. And God isn't a respecter of persons. You may not commit the same sin as another person, but sin is still sin.

You see, we have a tendency to want to put the guilt on the other fellow — he's so bad, but we're not so bad. And yet all of us have sinned and come short of the glory of God. We've all broken the Law in some little point. None of us has anything to brag about! Thank God for His mercy and forgiveness.

Now if James 2:10 isn't so, then let's just tear that page out. However, if you start tearing pages out of the Bible, before you know it, you won't have anything left.

It's like the little girl who went to church, and after the service her pastor was standing at the door shaking hands with the folks. She had her Sunday school book and the covers of her Bible under her arm. The pastor shook her hand and then looked at those Bible covers. He thought maybe they'd just come loose from the pages.

He said to her, "Honey, you don't have anything in your Bible but the backs. Did you lose all the pages?"

She said, "No, I didn't lose them. But every time you told us something that wasn't for us today, I tore the page out. So now all I've got left are the backs, and I'm expecting to get rid of them today."

That's getting right down to the truth about how some ministers preach! But, you see, God's Word *is* for us today! And Jesus Christ has already paid for every one of our sins — big and small!

Therefore, if you are going to succeed in God, you've got to forgive yourself for all your past mistakes and failures. Who is there of us that hasn't failed? Do you know anyone?

Some folks say, "Well, *I* believe in living above sin." I do too, but I don't know anyone who has done that yet. We're all still working on it. The only perfect Person I know was Jesus, and they crucified Him for it.

Then other people say, "Well, just go ahead and sin all you want to because God will forgive you." I doubt very seriously that folks who say things like that have ever been born again, because when you're born again, your nature is changed. You've got the love of God in your heart, and you don't want to do what's wrong.

As long as you are walking in love, you won't be willfully sinning. But every step out of love is sin. Many times we sin by not walking in love, and we don't even realize it.

For example, we haven't realized as we should have that forgiving *but not forgetting* is not walking in love. It is sin to hold on to other people's mistakes — or even your own.

Aren't you glad that we've got the Word! Aren't you glad that we can walk in the light of the Word! The psalmist of old said, *"The entrance of thy words giveth light. . ."* (Ps. 119:130). Once we have God's light on the matter of forgiveness, we can forgive ourselves and put our past in the sea of forgetfulness.

Paul Had To Forgive Himself

I want to look in the Bible at someone who had to forgive himself. The Apostle Paul was writing to the church at Philippi when he penned these words.

PHILIPPIANS 3:12-14
12 Not as though I had already attained, EITHER WERE ALREADY PERFECT: but I follow after, if that I may apprehend that for which also I am apprehended of Christ Jesus.
13 Brethren, I count not myself to have apprehended: but this one thing I do, FORGETTING THOSE THINGS WHICH ARE BEHIND, and reaching forth unto those things which are before,

14 I press toward the mark for the prize of the high calling of God in Christ Jesus.

Paul himself said that he didn't count himself to be already perfect or mature yet. That word "perfect" means *fully mature* or *mature in character*.

In other words, Paul wasn't perfected in love yet. If Paul hadn't yet attained perfection in love but kept on pressing toward that goal, then we're in good company, because we are also pressing on toward spiritual maturity in Christ.

None of us is perfect or fully mature in love yet, but that's what we are all striving toward. But, thank God, we can grow and develop in love! We are still pressing forward toward the mark for the prize of the high calling of God in Christ Jesus.

I want you to notice two things in particular in this passage of Scripture in Philippians. Paul had to *forget* those things which were behind, including his past mistakes and failures. And then he had to reach forth unto those things which were before him.

There is a spiritual truth here. Before you can go on with God, you have to learn to forget about your past mistakes.

Paul wrote this to the Philippian Church. That means before he could write these words to someone else, he had to practice this truth himself. Why would Paul have to forgive himself? Did Paul do anything in his past that he was ashamed of? Read what He said about himself when he wrote to Timothy.

1 TIMOTHY 1:11-16
11 According to the glorious gospel of the blessed God, which was committed to my trust.
12 And I thank Christ Jesus our Lord, who hath enabled me, for that he counted me faithful, putting me into the ministry;
13 WHO WAS BEFORE A BLASPHEMER, AND A PERSECUTOR, AND INJURIOUS: but I obtained mercy, because I did it ignorantly in unbelief.
14 And the grace of our Lord was exceeding abundant with faith and love which is in Christ Jesus.
15 This is a faithful saying, and worthy of all acceptation, that Christ Jesus came into the world to save sinners; of whom I am chief.
16 Howbeit FOR THIS CAUSE I OBTAINED MERCY, that in me first Jesus Christ might shew forth all longsuffering, for a pattern to them which should hereafter believe on him to life everlasting.

Before his conversion, Saul, later called Paul, persecuted and injured the Early Church. Paul says that he was a blasphemer, a persecutor, and injurious to others.

For example, the Bible says that Saul consented to Stephen's death (Acts 8:1). And when the persecutors of the Early Church stoned Stephen, they laid their clothes down at Saul's feet (Acts 7:58).

Then in Acts chapter 9, we read another account of Saul's persecution of the Early Church and his subsequent conversion.

ACTS 9:1-6
1 And SAUL, YET BREATHING OUT THREATENINGS AND SLAUGHTER AGAINST THE DISCIPLES OF THE LORD, went unto the high priest,

2   And desired of him letters to Damascus to the synagogues, THAT IF HE FOUND ANY OF THIS WAY, whether they were men or women, HE MIGHT BRING THEM BOUND UNTO JERUSALEM.
3   And as he journeyed, he came near Damascus: and suddenly there shined round about him a light from heaven:
4   And he fell to the earth, and heard a voice saying unto him, SAUL, SAUL, WHY PERSECUTEST THOU ME?
5   And he said, Who art thou, Lord? And the Lord said, I AM JESUS WHOM THOU PERSECUTEST: it is hard for thee to kick against the pricks.
6   And he trembling and astonished said, Lord, what wilt thou have me to do? And the Lord said unto him, Arise, and go into the city, and it shall be told thee what thou must do.

By reading these passages of Scripture, you can see that Paul had a lot to forget! He not only persecuted believers — but according to verse 5, Paul was really persecuting Jesus! That's one reason Paul said, "Forgetting the things that are behind, I press toward the mark. . . ."

It was a terrible thing for Paul to remember the havoc he'd wrought in the Church. He not only consented to Stephen's death, but the Bible says that he also breathed out threatenings and slaughter and locked many believers up in prison.

After Paul's conversion, before he could walk on with God, he had to learn to forget his past mistakes, including his terrible persecution of Christians. In order to stand in the full potential of the office and ministry God had called him to, Paul had to forget his past and forgive himself!

The same thing is true for you. If you don't learn to forgive yourself and forget your past mistakes, you'll be hindered in doing what God has called you to do.

You not only have to learn to forgive others — you have to learn to forgive yourself! And realize that very closely associated with learning to forgive is learning to forget.

If you keep hanging on to the past, you'll be handicapped all the rest of your life in living for God. You won't be able to be a successful Christian if you're always looking backward.

If you've asked forgiveness and God doesn't remember your past, why should you? When you condemn yourself and constantly feel guilty, your faith won't work.

Well, all of us are sorry when we miss it. If we are really walking with God, none of us wants to miss it. But we are still human, and we do miss it from time to time. But that's why we need a Savior! That's why we need Jesus!

Look at something John said in his epistle.

1 JOHN 4:7-12
7   Beloved, let us love one another: for love is of God; and every one that loveth is born of God, and knoweth God.
8   He that loveth not knoweth not God; for God is love.
9   In this was manifested the love of God toward us, because that God sent his only begotten Son into the world, that we might live through him.

10 Herein is love, not that we loved God, but that he loved us, and SENT HIS SON TO BE THE PROPITIATION FOR OUR SINS.

11 Beloved, if God so loved us, we ought also to love one another.

12 No man hath seen God at any time. If we love one another, God dwelleth in us, and his love is perfected in us.

Look especially at verse 10: *"Herein is love, not that we loved God, but that he loved us, and sent his son to be the propitiation for our sins."*

God made Jesus to be the propitiation or the atonement for our sins. Therefore, the Bible says that if we confess our sins, God is faithful and just to forgive us our sins and to cleanse us from all unrighteousness (1 John 1:9).

That wasn't written to sinners; it doesn't belong to sinners. John was writing to Christians. John says, *"MY LITTLE CHILDREN, these things write I unto you, THAT YE SIN NOT. . ."* (1 John 2:1).

God doesn't want His children to sin. But then look at what the rest of that verse says, *". . . And if any man sin, we have an advocate with the Father, Jesus Christ the righteous."*

If we do miss it and sin, we have an advocate with God — Jesus Christ the Righteous!

I've had people come up to me and say, "If you teach people this, you're going to give them a license to sin."

I always say, "They don't need a license; they'll do enough sinning without a license!"

We can be glad we have an Advocate with the Father — and He is Jesus Christ the Righteous! An advocate means a lawyer or one who pleads our case or our cause before God the righteous Judge.

The next verse may cause you to shout.

> **1 JOHN 2:2**
> **2   And HE** [Jesus] **IS THE PROPITIATION FOR OUR SINS: and not for ours only, but also for the sins of the whole world.**

Notice that the Bible differentiates between the sins of Christians and the sins of the whole world. That's because Christians have an Advocate with the Father — Jesus Christ the Righteous. They can appropriate First John 1:9 and come boldly before the Father and receive forgiveness of sins.

But the sinner in the world can't do that. In order to deal with his sin, the sinner must first receive Jesus Christ as his Savior.

Thank God, Jesus is the propitiation for our sins. Now I said that so you will forgive yourself and get healed if you need it, and forgive yourself so you can go on with your life.

Remember, dear friends, if you're going to go on with God and be successful in your Christian life and ministry, you need to learn how to forget! If you don't learn the lesson of forgetting your past mistakes, you'll be spiritually crippled in life.

Take God at His Word

I was holding a meeting in Texas, and a woman stopped me after the service and said, "I want you to pray for me."

"What for?" I asked.

She asked, "Do I have to tell you?"

I said, "I'm not going to pray for you unless you do."

After all, if people want me to pray for them, they're expecting me to have faith for whatever I'm praying for. I can't have faith for something if I don't know what I'm supposed to be believing for.

So she said, "Well, I've been saved for eight years and baptized with the Holy Ghost. My husband is not saved, and every once in a while, he will take a drink. He is a good man, and he loves me, and we have a good marriage.

"Well, awhile back, he came home and acted like he was drunk. I always was hot-tempered, and before I knew it, I let my temper get away from me. I lost my temper and said things I shouldn't have said.

"My husband said, 'Oh, I'm not drunk. I was just putting on. I just had one drink. I thought it would be funny just to come in and act like I was drunk.'

"Well, that made me madder than ever. I went to my room and slammed the door, and it took me a couple of hours to cool off. Afterwards, the words I said kept coming back to me.

"I thought, *I didn't say that, did I!* Then I got embarrassed. My husband is not even a Christian, and here I am saved and filled with the Holy Ghost, flying off the handle and saying things that weren't right.

"Well, I repented and spent the whole night on my knees, asking God to forgive me. I teach Sunday school, and here I had to go teach Sunday school the next morning!"

She continued, "At the breakfast table the next morning, I asked my husband to forgive me. He said, 'You don't have to ask me to forgive you. I ought to ask you to forgive me, since I'm the one who was wrong.'"

I said, "Sister, you haven't given me a prayer request. You've just told me something."

She said, "Here's the prayer request. I know God said that if we confess our sins, He will forgive us. But I want you to pray that God would give me some kind of a feeling so I would know He has forgiven me."

I said, "Sister, do you know what you just got through telling me? You just got through telling me that you have more faith in your unsaved husband than you do in God.

"You believed your husband when he said he forgave you, but you don't believe God when He said in His Word that He forgave you!"

She said, "Well, I know my husband. I know he really meant it."

I said, " You can take your husband at his word, but you can't take God at His Word! You need to get acquainted with God!"

I told this sister, "You need to reverse that. You need to put the Word of God first. Your faith in God's Word comes second. And put your feelings last. Your feelings will eventually fall in line with what you believe — God's Word."

My faith is not in my feelings. I could care less how I feel. My faith is in what God said.

You see, God's Word works. But you'll have to be a doer of God's Word before it will work for you. Part of being a doer of God's Word is to forgive others and forgive yourself too.

God's Word works in every area of our lives. But you have to work it. It doesn't just work automatically. In other words, you have to act on it.

It's believing, acting on, and confessing God's Word that makes it work for you. You can't act on the Word and be a doer of God's Word if you aren't willing to forgive. It's absolutely impossible.

So learn to forgive so you can receive God's best in life. Practice what Paul did. Forget those things which are behind, and "press toward the mark for the prize of the high calling of God in Christ Jesus" (Phil. 3:14).

Chapter 5
The Benefits
Of Walking in Love

The Bible encourages us to make the love of God our great aim and our great quest in life (1 Cor. 14:1 *Amp.*). There must be a reason God wants walking in the God-kind of love to be a priority in our lives. Actually, there are wonderful benefits and good results that come when we walk in love.

For example, I have walked in divine health for more than sixty-five years. The last headache I had was in August 1933. Well, it's too late to start having headaches now! I'm not bragging on me; I'm bragging on Jesus and on His Word.

Now don't misunderstand me. I've passed up some marvelous opportunities. The last headache I can remember that tried to attach itself to me was in 1977. I had just pulled out into the street from our offices at RHEMA.

Suddenly my head started hurting. I said, "No, you don't, Satan! You have to leave in Jesus' Name." By the time I turned the corner, it was gone. That's the last time I can even remember passing up an opportunity to have a headache.

In all these years, I've never been sick unless I've missed it somewhere, either in the love walk or in obedience to God. Every step out of love is sin. Every single time I missed it, I repented just as fast as I could and got back into love and obedience.

Normally, the minute I repented, I was healed. I don't mean I had to wait several days for the symptoms to clear up. I was either immediately healed or well on the way to recovery.

For more than sixty years in the ministry, I have said that if my faith didn't work and my prayers weren't answered, unforgiveness is the first place I would look. I'm not saying that *all* sickness and disease is caused by unforgiveness. I'm just saying that's the first place I would look.

Now don't misunderstand me at all. If folks need medicine, they should take medicine — under a doctor's supervision, of course. In fact, I've sent some folks to a doctor when they needed it and even bought them medicine. And if I needed an aspirin, I'd take it if I couldn't get healed any other way.

But, you see, the benefits of walking in love are so good, I want you to get in on them. The benefits include health and healing. The best time to get in on it is while you're young, so you can enjoy the blessings and the benefits of walking in the God-kind of love all the rest of your life.

I'm very careful about walking in love. Love is God's way to prosper — spirit, soul, and body. Walking in the God-kind of love is the way to prosper in every area of life. Love worketh what? Love worketh no ill to his neighbor. That means to anyone. And that should be especially true among Christians.

Walking in Love Is Profitable

Let's look at a verse of Scripture that talks about the rewards of walking in love. Walking in love is walking in godliness, isn't it? When you read this verse in First Timothy, substitute walking in the God-kind of love instead of the word "godliness."

> **1 TIMOTHY 4:8**
> **8 . . . Bodily exercise profits a little: BUT GODLINESS** [walking in love] **IS PROFITABLE UNTO ALL THINGS, having PROMISE of the life that now is, and of that which is to come.**

Paul, inspired by the Holy Spirit, wrote this to Timothy. This isn't just Paul speaking. This is not *man's* idea. The Holy Ghost said this to Christians everywhere through the Apostle Paul. *God* is telling us that godliness causes us to profit.

We would do no injustice to this Scripture to read it this way: "Walking in love is profitable unto all things." Why does the Bible say that bodily exercise only profits a little? Because it only has the promise of paying off in this life.

But the Bible says that godliness is profitable unto *all* things. When is godliness profitable? Is it only profitable when we get to Heaven? No, it's profitable in this life and also in the *next* life.

Therefore, godliness or walking in love is profitable throughout our lives. But if we live for God now and walk in the God-kind of love, it will also be profitable to us when we get to Heaven.

Living for God means keeping God's Word. If you're going to live for God, you've got to keep His commandments. Well, under the New Covenant, what commandments are you supposed to keep? There is only one, and it is the law of love!

Therefore, walking in the God-kind of love is profitable. Walking in love pays off. It pays off not only in this life, but also in the life to come.

Harboring Ill Will Damages *You!*

I've preached and practiced Mark 11:23 and 24 for more than fifty years. And I've acted on the spiritual truths Jesus quoted in these verses with amazing results.

But right along with Mark 11:23 and 24, I've also practiced verse 25 about forgiveness . All of my Christian life, I've always refused to harbor the least bit of animosity, ill will, or wrong feelings toward anyone.

If the least bit of ill will or animosity toward anyone tries to creep into my heart, I get after it! I won't entertain it for a moment. I wouldn't entertain that kind of wrong thinking any more than I would entertain the thought to steal from someone or to kill someone. Wrong feelings towards others *will do me damage*.

I would be just as careful about allowing unforgiveness and animosity in my heart toward another person as I would about drinking poison or handling a rattlesnake. Unforgiveness and wrong feelings toward others are more deadly than any poison or rattlesnake bite!

I believe that's one reason I've been able to walk in what I call divine health for many years. Now I'm not bragging on me. I'm bragging on Jesus and what the Word will do!

But that's why you'll never hear me criticize my brother or a fellow minister. No one has heard me criticize others in more than fifty years. I won't do it!

Sometimes I'll offer some *con*structive criticism. But, you see, *de*structive criticism is wrong. But constructive criticism is meant to help folks. And even if I do offer constructive criticism, I don't call anyone's name.

I'll tell you one thing about walking in God's best: If you want to walk in health, you are going to have to walk in love and keep your tongue!

Peter tells us how to practice what the Word says about walking in love.

1 PETER 3:8,9
8 Finally, be ye all of one mind, having compassion one of another, LOVE AS BRETHREN, be pitiful, be courteous:
9 Not rendering evil for evil, or railing for railing: but contrariwise blessing; knowing that ye are thereunto called, THAT YE SHOULD INHERIT A BLESSING.

The Amplified Bible says, ". . . sympathizing [with one another], loving [each the others] as brethren (of one household), compassionate and courteous — tenderhearted and humbleminded" (v. 8). That's the God-kind of love in action.

Keep Your Tongue So You Can Keep Your Life!

Sometimes it will take some effort on your part to walk in love. You'll have to keep your tongue under subjection to the man on the inside who is created in the image and likeness of God.

> **1 PETER 3:10,11**
> **10 For he that will love life, and see good days, LET HIM REFRAIN HIS TONGUE FROM EVIL, and his lips that they speak no guile** [deceit]**:**
> **11 LET HIM ESCHEW EVIL, and do good; let him seek peace, and ensue it**

Peter was quoting Psalm 34 when he said that. The psalmist knew that he would have to keep his tongue from evil so his voice would be heard on High.

> **PSALM 34:12-15**
> **12 What man is he that desireth life, and loveth MANY DAYS, that he may see GOOD?**
> **13 KEEP THY TONGUE FROM EVIL, and THY LIPS FROM SPEAKING GUILE.**
> **14 Depart from evil, and do good; seek peace, and pursue it.**
> **15 The EYES OF THE LORD ARE UPON THE RIGHTEOUS, and HIS EARS ARE OPEN UNTO THEIR CRY.**

Have you ever stopped to think that your tongue has a lot to do with the quality of your life? It also has a lot to do with how long you live on this earth! And it has much to do with whether or not the days you live are good days or bad days. What you say has everything in the world to do with enjoying a long, *good* life!

The secret of enjoying life and seeing many long, *good* days is contained in First Peter 3:10: *". . . refrain your tongue from evil. . . ."* Love always refrains from talking evil. Love speaks no guile or evil about others, and the God-kind of love seeks peace with every person.

You won't be able to harbor unforgiveness in your heart and talk about others if you want to see many long, *good* days.

Those days when you are sick are not good days, are they? Sometimes when people are sick, even though they've been thoroughly grounded in the truth of the Word and they make all the right faith confessions, they have difficulty getting their faith to work for them.

They have faith, but they can't seem to get their faith activated. Well, why isn't it working? The first thing they should examine is their love walk. Are they harboring ill will or unforgiveness in their hearts? Are they speaking evil about others? Are they criticizing and backbiting others?

1 PETER 3:12
**12 For the eyes of the Lord are over THE RIGH-
TEOUS, and HIS EARS ARE OPEN UNTO THEIR
PRAYERS: but the face of the Lord is against them
that do evil.**

We could read this verse like this: "The eyes of the Lord are over those who do right." We could also read it like this: "The eyes of the Lord are over those who walk in love, and His ears are open to their prayers."

You see, there are no hindrances to your prayers when you're walking in the God-kind of love! But the Bible says, ". . . *the face of the Lord is against them that do evil.*" Every step out of love is sin. We could also read this verse, "The face of the Lord is against those who speak evil about others."

How does a Christian sin? By not walking in love. By talking about others. We could put it this way: Every step out of love is doing evil. Love worketh no ill to his neighbor. Love refrains from speaking evil. Love — God's love — would never say anything bad about anyone.

When you criticize others and speak evil about them, you are sinning because you're not walking in love.

I remember an incident that happened years ago when I was just a young man, and I was pastoring a little church in north Texas. In a large metropolitan city about forty-five miles away, one of the ministers got into some difficulty and was dismissed from his denomination.

Later during a sectional convention in our church, one of the district superintendents preached in the morning service and mentioned the situation. Although he didn't call this minister's name, we all knew who he was talking about. He condemned him and just preached him right into hell, so to speak.

Well, some of the men who couldn't be in that morning service asked me about it later on. They asked, "Brother Hagin, what do you think about it? Was that minister right in what he said about that other minister?"

I said, "Yes, I concurred with him."

Well, about two weeks after that, my wife's parents came down to visit us. They lived out on a farm about forty miles away. My wife and two children went home with them after the Sunday night service. I was going to drive up there and join them after I attended to some church business.

So my wife and our children were gone, and I was alone in the parsonage. I listened to the news on the radio (we didn't have television back then).

The parsonage was an old house that was built before in-door electricity was available. When it was wired for electricity, they just put a chain hanging right down in the middle of the room to turn the light on and off.

When I was ready to go to bed, I just reached up to turn the light off and then knelt by the foot of the bed and prayed. Suddenly the whole room lit up! The Bible talks about a light Paul saw that was brighter than the noonday sun (Acts 9:3; 22:6). This light was bright like that. The whole room lit up brighter than when the light was on, and I could see every piece of furniture.

And then out of the bright light I heard these words, "Who art thou that condemneth another man's servant?" I knew it was the Lord.

I said, "Lord, I didn't condemn Your servant." I knew immediately who the Lord was referring to. He was talking about that minister who'd gotten into trouble.

The Lord answered me again by saying, "Who art thou that condemneth another man's servant?"

I repeated, "Lord, I never condemned Your servant."

Then the third time the Lord said, "Who art thou that condemneth another man's servant?"

I said the third time, "Lord, I didn't condemn Your servant."

The Lord said, "Didn't you say. . . ," and then the Lord quoted what I had said about this minister.

Well, you get in a situation like that and your flesh sometimes wants to take over. You remember when Adam got into trouble, he wanted to shift the blame to the woman. Then when that didn't work, he said, "This woman which *Thou* gavest me." Really, he was trying to blame everyone else so he wouldn't have to be responsible. The flesh always wants to blame someone else.

I said, "Lord, I was just quoting the district superintendent."

The Lord said to me, "When you repeated it, that was tantamount to your saying it. Who art thou that condemneth another man's servant?"

When the Lord said that, He just sort of knocked the props out from under me. So then I said, "I thought that minister was wrong. I mean, didn't he do wrong?"

The Lord never told me whether he'd done wrong or not. But He asked me a question. He said, "Whose servant is he, Mine or yours?"

I said, "If he is anyone's servant, Lord, he's Yours. He sure isn't mine."

The Lord said, "Well, if he is My servant, then I'm able to make him stand." And, you know, the Lord did just that. The Lord made the man stand, and that fellow went on to become the most outstanding minister in that part of the state. He was very well respected, even though he'd missed it that one time in his past.

Who are we to criticize the Lord's servants! Sometimes it's the things we say about other people that cause us ill health.

I had another experience along this same line. My wife and I held a meeting down in east Texas in a Full Gospel church. We were going from that meeting to a convention that our denomination was holding.

One of the ministers in that part of the state had gotten into some difficulty, and he had to leave the church. I asked someone, "What did he do?" And the person told me what the minister had done.

Well, without thinking, I just said, "It looks to me like anybody with any sense would know better than to do that." I never thought anything else about it. My wife and I closed that meeting, and we went on our way to the convention.

Now ordinarily I walk in divine health; I just feel good all the time. But during this convention, I just wasn't up to par physically, and I couldn't sleep at night. Normally by the time my head hits the pillow, I'm asleep.

I made all the right faith confessions, and I believed I received my healing, but I still didn't feel good physically. On the third night of the convention, I still couldn't sleep. I said, "Lord, if I'm feeling like this tomorrow, I won't be able to go to the meetings. My body is about to give out."

I got out of bed and got on my knees and started praying. I remembered something Dr. Lilian B. Yeomans said. She was a medical doctor who at one time had become addicted to drugs. She became sick and really just went down to death's door. But then she got saved and God raised her up from a deathbed. She then spent the rest of her life preaching about divine healing.

Dr. Yeomans said, "If I pray and don't get results, *I* start changing. Why? Because there will have to be a change somewhere before the answer can come, and the change won't be with God, because God never changes."

I remembered reading this statement by Dr. Yeomans, so I started changing. I'd been making all the right biblical confessions and saying all the right things, but I still hadn't improved.

Finally, I said to the Lord, "Lord, what is wrong with me? I haven't made my faith connection with You."

The Lord spoke to me and said, "Didn't you say so and so about Brother _____," and the Lord called this pastor's name.

I said, "Lord, all I said was 'It looks like anybody with any sense would have known better than to do that.'"

The Lord asked me a question. He said, "Do you know what pressure he was under?"

I said, "No."

The Lord asked me, "Do you know the circumstances that surrounded this situation?"

I said, "No."

The Lord said to me, "If you'd been in the same position, you might not have done as well as he did."

With tears, I said, "Oh, God, forgive me. My God, please forgive me. I repent."

Do you know that as soon as I repented, I was instantly well. It didn't take me time to get healed — I was instantly made whole! I got into bed and slept soundly for the first time in several nights.

You see, there's a principle here. We can't criticize and judge the other fellow because we don't know the circumstances and the pressures that the person may have been under that caused him to act as he did. We don't know what made him do what he did — only the Lord knows.

It's situations like this that taught me to keep my mouth shut about criticizing the Lord's servants. It's so easy to criticize the other fellow. But we may not have done as well as he did under the same circumstances. The Bible says, *"Judge not, that ye be not judged"* (Matt. 7:1). That's why we can't judge, or we will be judged by the Lord.

There are some believers who are always criticizing others and spreading gossip. For example, someone once said to me, "Did you hear what happened? That preacher had an affair with his secretary."

"He did? But it looks like God is really blessing him and his church. When did this happen?"

"Oh, about twelve years ago."

"Then why are you talking about it now! That shouldn't be told about him. That's a lie the devil told on him because that man repented and got right with God. So that sin has been blotted out by the blood of Jesus.

"It's in the sea of forgetfulness. God forgot about it, and if you're going to walk in love, you've got to forget about it, too, and not go around talking about it!"

Did you ever read in the Bible where it said, *"And above all things have fervent charity among yourselves: for charity shall cover the multitude of sins"* (1 Peter 4:8). It also says, *"Hatred stirreth up strifes: but love covereth all sins"* (Prov. 10:12).

Love is not out uncovering sins; love covers sin. I pastored nearly twelve years. I saw certain things about certain church members, but I never told anyone, not even my wife. Why? Because it may have damaged them.

You may say, "But they did wrong." But most of the time those folks came to themselves and said, "Dear Lord! How did I get into this? Lord, please forgive me." And they got right back out of it.

But if I'd gone and told it, then everyone would know, and every time they looked at the person, they'd think about that. And then the devil would try to bring it to their remembrance too. No! Love *covers* a multitude of sins!

But so many times *people* have a hard time forgiving and forgetting. For example, I was holding a crusade in a certain city when news broke out about a certain minister. Someone asked me what I thought about it.

He asked, "What do you think about what happened to So-and-so?"

I just said, "I have no comment."

"Oh, really?" he said.

Then I added, "Putting out the other fellow's candle never brightens your own."

I'm not going to put anyone's candle out. I'm going to try to light it if I can! Dear friends, if we want to walk with God, we've got to walk in love because God *is* love!

I remember once my wife and I held a meeting in our home church in McKinney, Texas. An older gentleman we knew named Brother Smith came to the meeting. As a young Baptist boy preacher, I had supplemented my income by working for him.

Brother Smith told me after the service, "Brother Kenneth, I always enjoyed hearing you speak because you preach faith and healing."

Then he said, "You know, I haven't been sick for forty years, and I'll be ninety years old next month.

Forty years ago, someone came to our church preaching about divine healing.

"That minister had those of us in the congregation come down front and accept Christ as our Physician, just like we accepted Him as our Savior. I marched down to the altar and accepted Jesus as both my Savior and my Physician. And now physically I am just as good a man at ninety as I was at twenty-one years of age."

Brother Smith continued, "For one thing, I work every day." He was quite wealthy, and he didn't have to work at all, but he did.

Then he said, "And after I accepted Christ as my Savior, I read in the Bible where it says, ". . . *the very hairs of your head are all numbered*" (Matt. 10:30).

I said, "Lord, if You know how many hairs I have, then You can keep my hair too!"

Then he added, "Brother Kenneth, I also believed God to keep my teeth!" And he opened his mouth and showed me. He didn't have one single filling! At ninety years old, he still had all his teeth!

He continued, "But I'll tell you one thing! I also prayed that God would help me keep this!" and he stuck his tongue out. He said, "I saw that if I was going to have divine health, I would have to keep *this*!"

When Brother Smith said that, I remembered an incident that had happened when I had worked for him before World War II. There was a fellow in town who was a World War I veteran. He'd been gassed in the war, and he would have spells where he would go crazy and start cutting people up with a knife.

The whole town of about 9,000 people knew about his condition and sympathized with him because he was a veteran and had been afflicted serving his country in the war.

When he would get on one of these spells, the fellow would spend a night or so in jail, then they'd let him out, and he'd be all right for a while. Even those he'd attacked wouldn't press charges against him because they knew what he'd gone through in the war.

But one Saturday night, the chief of police was called to come over and get this fellow because none of the other policemen could handle him. When that fellow would get drunk, the chief of police could always talk him out of getting violent and take him to jail to sleep it off so he could get over it.

But this Saturday night when the chief was called, the man wouldn't put his knife away. The poor fellow had suffered so much, and his mind was not right. He really just wanted to die.

The man said to the police chief, "Either I'm going to cut your throat, or you're going to kill me — one of the two." Saying that, the man lunged at the chief with a knife, leaving him no choice but to shoot him. And the man died about four o'clock the next morning in the hospital.

The next day news of his death went all over town, and everyone was talking about it. Almost the whole town sighed in relief that he was dead. People said many things about it, but I noticed that Brother Smith would not say anything about it.

Some people said, "They should have put the so-and-so in the electric chair!"

It seemed like everyone had something bad to say about him. When everyone got through talking about the man, Brother Smith said, "One thing I noticed — he surely had pretty eyes." When Brother Smith said that, everyone just hushed and walked away. Brother Smith would never say one bad word against anyone.

As Brother Smith talked to me that day years later, I remembered that incident. Here Brother Smith was ninety years old and still in good health because he'd learned the secret of keeping his tongue from speaking evil and walking in love.

You see, God didn't just look down from Heaven, and say, "Let's make an example of that man named Smith down there in Collin County, Texas, and give him a long, good life!"

No, Brother Smith had something to do with that! He had read in the Bible about keeping his tongue from evil so he could see many *good* days full of life. To do that, he had to walk in love by keeping his tongue and by forgiving others!

Thank God for the Word! If it's your desire to have a long, good life, then keep your tongue from evil. Depart from evil — not just in speaking evil — but *you* depart from evil in every area of your life and do good. Then not only *seek* peace with everyone around you, but *pursue* peace (Ps. 34:12-14).

What does this have to do with walking in love? It has everything to do with it! God knew we would have to forgive one another. That's why He told us to pursue peace with all people.

Also, remember, this passage in Ephesians was written to church people!

EPHESIANS 4:32
32 And BE YE KIND ONE TO ANOTHER, TEN-DERHEARTED, FORGIVING ONE ANOTHER, even as God for Christ's sake hath forgiven you.

EPHESIANS 5:1,2
1 Be ye therefore followers of God as dear chil-dren:
2 And WALK IN LOVE, AS CHRIST ALSO HATH LOVED US, and hath given himself for us an offer-ing and a sacrifice to God for a sweetsmelling savour.

Think about it. There would be no need for God to tell us to forgive one another if there was nothing to for-give. Many times, there's plenty to forgive, isn't there? That's why God told us to be kind, tenderhearted, and forgiving of one another. He knew we would have many opportunities in which we would have to exercise the God-kind of love and forgive.

For example, do some people's personalities just seem to rub your "fur" the wrong way? Do some people just seem to grate on you? Well, if they do, you can't let that bother you. You just have to forgive them, love them anyway, and keep a good report. Otherwise, it will hinder your faith and can even cause you to get sick.

Divine Love vs. Human Love

Not only is the love of God forgiving, God's love is also unselfish. God's love thinks of others first. On the other hand, the flesh is selfish and self-centered. Human love puts itself first.

Sometimes I think that some people get this love business all mixed up. When some Christians talk about love, they are thinking about natural human love. They try to compare divine love with natural human love, and you can't compare human love with divine love. We're not talking about natural human love. We are talking about divine love.

The Bible said, "God is love." Well, God is divine. God is love. God is not anything so much as He is love.

We hear a lot today about natural human love, but there is no love in all the world like the love of God. Natural human love is selfish and self-centered.

I remember a woman came up to me in a meeting I was holding in a church. She said, crying, "God knows I love my children.

"I brought them up right, but not one of them will come to church with me except my daughter." Her daughter played the piano at that church.

She said, "There isn't anyone in all this church that has loved their children as much as I have loved mine."

Well, I could look at her daughter playing the piano and see that something was wrong with her. She was about twenty-four years old, and she'd taken music lessons and had even been to college. But if you looked at her, she'd duck her head to hide from you.

I said to her mother, "When your daughter was growing up, did you ever allow her to have friends? She must be intelligent because she made good grades in college and she graduated with a degree in music." I knew a little bit about the family from what the pastor had told me.

I asked this mother, "Did you ever permit her to have a boyfriend or a friend at school?"

"No," her mother answered, "I just kept her at home. I wanted to protect her because I love her so much."

I said, "You're lying. You didn't keep her at home because you loved her so much. You kept her at home because your love is selfish." I know that's not the way to win friends, but sometimes you have to jolt people to get them to see the truth!

"Well, I just love her too much to let her go," the mother said to me. "She's never been away from home one night in her life."

I said, "No, you don't love her. You love her with selfish human love. If you really loved your children with the God-kind of love, you'd want them to have friends. You'd want them to mix with people their own age and grow up and live a normal life."

Then she said, "My son is seventeen years old, and he just ran off from home. I don't know where he is. Pray that he'll come back."

I said, "No! I'm going to pray that he'll stay gone. Thank God, he had enough sense to get up and get out of that mess. That poor girl sitting over there at the piano stool probably hasn't got that much sense because you've warped her personality."

You see, here was a woman who was born again and even filled with the Spirit and attended a Full Gospel church, but she really didn't love her children with the divine love of God at all. She loved them with a natural human love, and that can be selfish.

Believers can't say, "But it's impossible for me to love with God's love," because the Bible says that God's love is already in our hearts in the new birth. Everyone in the family of God has it, or else they haven't been born again.

Now they may not be *exercising* God's love, but they have it. They just have to learn to let that divine love dominate them. If they would learn to walk in love, they would walk in the Spirit because love is a fruit of the recreated human spirit.

If we would learn to walk in love and let that divine love dominate us, it would make all the difference in our lives. It would cure the ills in our homes.

I'm going to say something that may shock you but it's true: Divine love has never been to a divorce court, and it never will. Natural, human love will go to the divorce court, but divine love won't — and it will never fail.

You see, my friends, the God-kind of love is not self-seeking. Divine love is interested in what it can *give*,

not in what it can *get*. It's not selfish or self-seeking.
Divine love doesn't ask, "What can I get?" It asks,
"What can I give?"

Human love is interested in *self* — "What will *I* get
out of this situation." Human, selfish love says things
like, "I'm not going to take that!" Or "I'm going to have
my way! After all, I've got my say-so." Self-centered
Christians are very easy to locate: "I . . . ," "I . . . ,"
"I . . . ." All they ever talk about is "I."

Too many Christians are selfish. They let natural
human love dominate them instead of the love of God
which has been shed abroad in their spirit — their
heart.

Natural human love will divide homes, and it will
divide churches because it's selfish and it wants its own
way.

Did you ever stop to think about it? Selfishness
ruins the world. Selfishness ruins marriages, and it
ruins the church. But the God-kind of love never fails
because it's unselfish, and it always puts the other fellow first.

God's love is giving, and the God-kind of love thinks
of other people first, just as God did: "God so loved the
world that He *gave*. . ." (John 3:16). When sinners in
the world were unlovely, God *gave* His only begotten
Son, ". . . *that whosoever believeth in him should not
perish, but have everlasting life"* (John 3:16).

But, you see, we human beings get our feelings
hurt, and then we want to strike back and retaliate

instead of exercising forgiveness. Our feelings want to show up and our flesh wants to act up.

That's what the Word means when it says we have to "crucify the flesh" (Gal. 5:24). I don't know about you, but I refuse to get hurt feelings about anything.

Some say, bawling, squalling, and carrying on, "But you don't know how bad you hurt me!" That's selfishness showing up, not the God-kind of love, because you're only thinking about yourself. When you talk like that, you're allowing your flesh and your feelings to dominate you.

When your feelings dominate you, you're going to have to get out of the flesh and get into the Spirit so you can walk in the God-kind of love! The Bible says, *". . . ye are not in the flesh, but IN THE SPIRIT, if so be that the Spirit of God dwell in you. . ."* (Rom. 8:9).

Come on over and walk in the Spirit! Come up higher and walk in the God-kind of love! It's so much better. And I'll tell you, it pays rich dividends!

If you want to love life and see many good days, you'd better listen! Thank God, the love of God works.

Someone said, "But I've failed so much in the past!" Well, if you've failed in the past, then ask God's forgiveness and put that all behind you. Start over in the present! One thing about it, God will let you start all over again because in His great mercy and in His great love, He is forgiving!

Aren't you glad God is that way? God said, *"I, even I, am he that blotteth out thy transgressions for mine own sake, and will not remember thy sins"* (Isa. 43:25).

So even if you do miss it, if you repent, God will forgive you, blot it out, and not even remember that you did anything wrong! So start walking in His forgiveness and mercy and get on with your life.

Divine Love Can Be Stern

You see, when we talk about love, we're talking about the God-kind of love — divine love. Too many times I think people try to compare divine love with natural human love. But divine love and natural love are entirely different.

Natural human love can change and turn to hatred overnight. Or it can be soft and mushy sometimes when it should be firm and sometimes even stern. But sometimes divine love can be very stern. You see, there's another side to God's love.

For example, was Jesus a Man of love when He walked on this earth? Of course He was. He was also a Man of faith, power, and a Man of God! He was tempted in all points just like we are, yet He never committed a sin. He was the only Man who never sinned.

But remember when He took that whip and drove those money changers out of the temple? Was He acting in love? Yes, He was. You see, there's a stern side to love. God is love, and there's a gracious, gentle side of God. But there is also a stern, judgmental side of God's love.

It's just like the love parents have toward their children. Sometimes parents have to reprimand their children and be very stern with them. Do they discipline their children because they hate them? No, they discipline them because they love them.

People have quoted for years, "Spare the rod and spoil the child." Did you know that is not in the Bible? Actually, the Bible is tougher than that. It says, *"He that spareth his rod hateth his son: but he that loveth him chasteneth him betimes"* (Prov. 13:24). In other words, if you love your children, you will discipline them.

Sometimes love — the God-kind of love — has to be stern too. Let me show you what I mean. My wife and I went to pastor a church in 1946. When we first got there, I don't think there were any young people at all in that particular church who were saved, and the teenagers would misbehave in church.

In those days, we only had a small, one-room auditorium. There weren't any nurseries or other rooms, not even a prayer room, but the sanctuary seated about 300 people.

The teenagers would sit on the back pew, and they'd talk, laugh, and carry on out loud during the church services. They were talking so loudly that I could hear them when I was trying to preach!

Then sometimes we would have visiting singers who would sing a special song, and some of them even played the guitar too. These young people would sit in the back of the church and act up and pretend like they were playing a guitar, and they would sing louder than the guest singer.

Well, I knew enough to know that you just can't go into a new place and start changing things overnight. So I put up with it for several months, trying to work with the people just saying things like, "We're going to have order in the services!"

One Sunday night I was preaching, and the sanctuary was just packed. The windows were open, and sometimes there were more people standing outside looking in the windows listening to the sermon than there were inside the building.

Two young men, who were strangers to our church, were talking so loudly in the back of the church that the people in the front row turned around and looked at them.

Finally, I stopped right in the middle of my sermon, closed my Bible, and said, "That's it!" I didn't want to embarrass those fellows because they were new to the church, so I asked, "Is somebody talking?"

Someone in the congregation answered, "Yes."

I said, "Now I've talked to you very kindly for more than three months about not talking during the message and keeping order in the service. But from this moment on, the next person who talks out loud in church or disturbs the service in any way, I'm going to have arrested for disturbing public worship!"

Someone spoke up and said, "We've heard that before!" I said, "Yes, and now you're going to see it!" Then I dismissed the service. There was no use preaching; the service had already been disrupted.

I learned later that some of the former pastors had even gone so far as to have some people arrested for disturbing the services. But they wouldn't prefer charges against them, so the people were let go.

I began to go talk to the parents of the children who were making such a disturbance. First I went to Brother H_____ who had two teenaged daughters.

I said to him, "Now Brother H_____, I'm going to have your two daughters arrested for disturbing public worship if they keep it up. And you'll either have to pay their fine or else they'll have to work it out on the county farm."

In those days, you could work your fine out on the county farm. I thought he would oppose me for saying that, but he said to me, "Brother Hagin, you're exactly right. I say go ahead and have them arrested. I can't pay the fine, so they'll just have to work it out on the county farm."

He added, "You know, I've told them again and again, 'If you can't behave in church, don't go down there.' You may wonder why I, a man who is 6 feet 4 inches tall, can't handle two teenaged daughters. But my main trouble is my wife, because she won't cooperate with me."

When a couple won't work together in an attitude of love to raise their children, it makes a big problem and creates a mess.

I went to another dear lady, bless her heart, and I said to her, "Have your children sit up on the front row with you so you can watch them and make them behave."

She said, "But Brother Hagin, if I have my children sit with me, I can't really get into the service and shout and dance and carry on."

I told her, "You will be a greater blessing to this church if you would make your kids mind you than if you're dancing and shouting."

Then I went to talk to another parent, Mr. H_____. He wasn't a Christian, but his wife was a member of the church. He'd bring their boys to church, but he'd just stand outside the church building with them and not come in.

But his daughters would come into the sanctuary, and they always talked and carried on. I took two of the deacons with me as witnesses when I went to talk to this man because he wasn't a Christian.

I said, "Mr. H_____, I'm going to have your daughters arrested for disturbing public worship if they keep acting up. But I wanted to be fair about it and come and talk to you first. If they keep on disturbing the service, you'll either have to pay their fine, or else they'll have to work their fine out on the county farm."

He threatened me by saying, "Well, you and these deacons aren't always on this church property!"

When he said that, I just stepped up almost in his face and said, "There's one thing about it. I'm not ashamed of *anything* or afraid of *anyone*!"

He backed down and said, "My girls are not the only ones who are acting up."

I told him, "No, they're not, but they're the worst ones."

And do you know that when he saw that I wasn't going to back down, he just changed and started talking kindly to me. Sometimes love has to be stern and fearless and not back down when it's in the right.

But do you know what happened in that church? Within six weeks, twenty-five of those same young people got saved and filled with the Holy Ghost. And they were the very ones who were doing all the talking!

You see, walking in the God-kind of love doesn't mean that you're milk-toast, and you just let everyone run over you. It doesn't mean that you have to be a doormat either, and just let people walk on you. But it does mean that you have to do what's right and sometimes that means not backing down.

In the early days of my ministry, I preached out in the country as a young Baptist boy preacher. I didn't have the baptism of the Holy Ghost at this particular time, although I was filled with the Spirit later on. I was eighteen, and I stayed at the home of some dear people who had two boys, one seventeen years old and one sixteen years old.

Both of these boys were bigger than I was. They were large, husky boys who'd been raised on the farm. I only weighed 138 pounds because I'd only been off the bed of sickness a couple of years.

The oldest boy, Ray, would throw mad fits, and he'd go through the house breaking up furniture. He'd slap his Momma around, and he'd usually grab a gun and go waving that around too.

I was staying with that family at this particular time because I was preaching in that town. One day this oldest boy came into my room in one of these mad fits, waving a gun and cussing at me.

I got right up in his face, and said, "Ray, wait a minute! Do you know who you're talking to! I'm the preacher in this town. Now I don't live here — this is not my house — but this is my room. You just be quiet and get out of here!"

Do you know that the minute I stood up to him, he just quieted right down. And he never came into my bedroom again. In fact, some time later after my wife and I got married, we went back to that same town and held a meeting and stayed with those same people.

And one time when we were staying there, Ray threw one of those fits, but he didn't dare come into our bedroom, even though it was years after that first incident. He just went through the house cussing everyone, but he didn't come into our room.

No, the God-kind of love doesn't mean that you just give in and let everyone walk all over you. On the other hand, it doesn't mean that you act up and bully everyone either. But sometimes the love of God means that you have to be stern and stand up for what you know is right.

God's love never fails! Therefore, if you are walking in His divine love, you can't fail. If you are walking in the God-kind of love, His love working in and through you will be more than enough for any situation.

The God-kind of love will put you over in life because God *is* love. And walking in God's love is profitable, not just in this life, but also in the life to come! Enjoy the benefits and great rewards of walking in the love of God.

CONFESSION:

I will walk in God's love. I will not criticize others because God's love works no ill to his neighbor.

When I am walking in God's love, I can claim God's best blessings in life. I will be tenderhearted and forgiving; therefore, I shall reap a blessing.

I will keep my tongue from speaking evil, and I will eschew evil and pursue peace with every man.

I thank You, Father, that as I endeavor to grow in the fruit of love, You will help me be all that I can be in You.

Chapter 6
Failing To Walk in Love Can Affect Your Health

If you're going to walk in divine health, you will have to walk in God's love. If your *faith* is going to work and be effectual, you will have to put the God-kind of love to work so *God's love* can be effectual.

God's love is the only thing that is going to win out in the end. Sometimes it will look like love is not winning, but if you just keep practicing it and exercising it, eventually it will win out in the end, because the Bible says love never fails.

Galatians 5:6 says, *"For in Jesus Christ neither circumcision availeth any thing, nor uncircumcision; but faith which worketh by love."* It is a scriptural principle that if you don't walk in love toward others, your faith won't work.

A Right Heart Receives From God

If only people understood how much walking in love has to do with folks receiving their healing. That's why in my meetings I encourage folks to hear as much of the Word as possible before they get into the healing line.

183

Sometimes they just need to make an adjustment in their love walk before they can receive their healing.

You see, sometimes by listening to the Word, people get to the root cause and find out where they are missing it in their faith connection. And a lot of times they are missing it in this area of walking in love and forgiveness.

Over the years, I've noticed that those folks who listen to the Word and respond to it by making the necessary adjustments in their heart are the ones who receive their healing. Only a small percentage of people receive healing who only go to one meeting, don't get into the Word for themselves, and don't make any needed changes.

For example, a woman came to my wife and me after a meeting once, and said, "I've had stomach trouble and a respiratory problem for some time. I decided to go to every one of your services and get in the healing line at the end of the week." She had already been to almost every leading healing evangelist in America at that time but had not been healed.

This woman said, "Toward the end of the week, I began to realize that before I could get into the healing line and expect God to do something for me, I was going to have to get my heart right by calling my brother to ask him to forgive me."

She went on to explain to my wife and me that she and her brother had had a disagreement twenty-five years before. They had not spoken to each other since, yet they both claimed to be Christians.

Folks ought to have enough sense to know that if they don't receive healing after hands have been laid on them a few times, particularly by those who are especially used by God along this line, they should look on the inside to see if they are out of line with God's Word somewhere. They should check up on themselves and start changing and making the necessary adjustments, because God never changes.

But too many times when folks don't get healed, they want to lay off all the responsibility on God or on someone else. But they need to check up on themselves first.

This woman checked up on the inside and realized she still harbored resentment and unforgiveness against her brother from something that had happened twenty-five years earlier.

She had recently been filled with the Holy Spirit, but she had been saved for many years. If she had been listening to her spirit, the Holy Ghost would have led her to reconcile with her brother years before. Sometimes it takes some people a long time to change, but it doesn't have to. They could change sooner if they would just learn to walk in love.

Anyway, she called her brother long distance, and said, "I just wanted to call and ask you to forgive me. I was wrong."

He said, "I'm so glad you called. I was thinking about calling you. You weren't to blame, I was. I've been intending to call you to ask you to forgive me."

They each finally agreed to take fifty percent of the blame. She told him that after the meeting, she was going to fly to New York to visit him.

She told me later that after she got things right with her brother, she felt a deep sense of peace and well-being on the inside. She lay down to take a nap before the evening service. Later she told my wife and me, "When I woke up, I couldn't find a trace of any kind of sickness. I mean, every symptom and every pain completely disappeared!"

She said, "I've never felt so good in all my life. All my stomach problems have disappeared, and so have my lung problems."

She said, "I came all the way down here to the meeting, and I never did get in the healing line. But when I forgave my brother and got things straightened out with him, I got healed!" The moment she started walking in love, she could claim God's promises about healing.

Over a period of many years, I've had person after person tell me that same thing — they had to forgive someone and get the situation straightened out before they could receive their healing. Some of them were even terminal cases.

One man told me, "My doctor said, 'You'll be dead in thirty days.'" The man just made the necessary adjustments in his heart by getting rid of every bit of ill will, animosity, and unforgiveness, and he's healed and still alive today.

I never did have to pray for him or lay hands on him. Think about that — he was healed of terminal cancer when he exercised forgiveness!

In more than half a century of ministry, I've dealt with thousands of people who needed healing — not all at one time, of course. But I'm talking about dealing with sick people on a one-to-one basis over a period of many years.

I've known people who got in the healing lines of nearly every leading evangelist of the day and still did not get well — especially in days gone by when there were healing revivals everywhere.

Then I've seen those same people make a trip to the prayer room and get their heart right with God Then you didn't even have to pray for them; their illnesses disappeared completely.

In my own ministry, I've had many people come forward in my healing lines who had been in everyone else's healing line in the country. They made a trip to the prayer room, got some things straightened out in their heart, and they were instantly healed.

They didn't have to get in *anyone's* prayer line. In fact, no one had to pray for them at all! They just got healed!

Some people are slow about catching on to the fact that faith simply will not work without love. People ought to know that if men of God — particularly those who are used of God along the line of healing — lay hands on them and they don't get any results, they ought to start examining themselves.

God doesn't ever change. Therefore, they are going to have to be the ones to change and make adjustments in their love walk.

You see, the Bible says it's the entrance of God's Word that gives light (Ps. 119:130). And when you walk in the light of that Word, you receive the results, the benefits, and the fruit thereof.

I've been in the healing ministry for nearly sixty years, and I know from experience that so many Christians fail to receive their healing because they're unwilling to straighten things up with others. They are unwilling to rid their heart of anything that isn't right with God.

Sometimes they need to forgive someone else, but sometimes they just need to forgive *themselves*. Some folks will forgive others, but not themselves. But they have to forgive themselves, too, in order to walk in health.

Harmful Effects of Animosity

Believers need to understand how much ill will and animosity will harm them. It can affect their spiritual growth, it can cause their prayers to be hindered, and it can even make them sick.

For example, when I was out in field ministry holding meetings, I happened to run into a pastor who had a church in that city. He didn't look well, so I asked him, "What's wrong with you?"

He asked me, "Do you know Brother So-and-so?"

I said, "Yes."

"Well," this pastor said, "he came into *my* town and started another church."

"*Your* town?" I asked.

"Yes."

"I didn't know this town belonged to you," I said.

"Well, I was the only Full Gospel church here," he said. "He did me wrong by starting another church here, and I will never forgive him for it."

Then he asked, "Kenneth, would you pray for me? I've got ulcers."

Well, I knew right then what had caused his ulcers. I knew it wouldn't do any good to pray for his healing because he still had animosity and unforgiveness in his heart. Besides, I happened to know that under all the rules of that pastor's particular denomination, the other pastor was perfectly within his rights to start a church in that city.

Not only that, but I knew something about the situation. Actually some other people started the church, not the other pastor. The people got together and said, "We want a church in our end of town," so they organized the church, got it started with sixty-seven people, and elected this new pastor.

That new pastor didn't even start that church. The people had even raised several thousand dollars, had bought a lot, and were ready to build a church building on it before the other pastor was even voted in to that church.

I said to this first pastor, "You ought to pray that God would send someone *else* into this town to start *another* church!"

Then I asked him, "How many people were you averaging in Sunday school before this other church started?"

He said, "About one hundred thirteen people, including kids, babies, and everyone."

I asked, "How many people are you averaging now in Sunday school?"

He said, "Oh, anywhere from two hundred forty to two hundred sixty people."

"How many is that other pastor averaging?"

"Well, I'm sorry to say, anywhere from two hundred sixty to two hundred eighty people. They're beating us!"

Can you imagine an attitude like that from a man of God! That wasn't the love of God in demonstration. No, it was selfish, human love showing up.

I said to him, "Whooo! Glory to God! Think about that! Here you are in this little ole town of fifteen hundred people, and in the last two years you are both reaching more than five hundred people every Sunday! You ought to pray another pastor into the east end of town. Then you ought to pray that someone would start a church in the north end of town."

"Yes, but this is *my* territory. He moved in on *my* territory. I just can't forgive him. I want to, but I can't. But I want you to pray for me."

I knew it wouldn't do any good to pray for his healing until he made an adjustment in his heart. It would have done no more good to pray for him than to say, "Twinkle, twinkle little star. How I wonder what you are."

Later, I heard that this pastor had been operated on for ulcers of the stomach. Soon after that I saw him again at a convention. He said, "I was operated on for ulcers of the stomach, but the ulcers have come back again. Would you pray for me?"

But I knew it wouldn't do any good to pray for his healing until he got that grudge out of his heart toward his brother and fellow minister. And thank God he did. When he finally repented for holding unforgiveness against this other pastor, he never had any more stomach problems, and he never had another operation. Those ulcers completely disappeared.

Love and forgiveness go hand in hand. You can't say you're walking in love if you harbor ill will in your heart.

Every step out of love is a step into sin. You can't walk in health and healing if you entertain unforgiveness or grudges in your heart. If you get out of the love walk, get back in just as fast as you can. Then you can live under God's abundant provision and promises and enjoy His best blessings in your life.

Not walking in love toward the brethren can affect your health. It can even shorten your life because it allows the devil a foothold in your life.

That's a solemn thought, isn't it? Well, we need to think soberly on the subject of love. After all, the Bible says that love is greater than faith or hope: *"And now abideth faith, hope, charity, these three; but the greatest of these is charity* [love]*"* (1 Cor. 13:13).

Love never fails. Love — God's divine love in us — can settle any quarrel or any dispute. It can solve any problem because God is love.

I've seen God's love work many times over the years.

You see, walking in love is an area of divine healing that needs to be preached too. Most of us want to live out our full length of time on this earth. Do you know it is possible for you to live out your full life on earth? The Bible promises that. But you'll have to walk in love and obedience to do it.

Do You Love Your Brother?

Ask yourself the question, *What have I done with the God-kind of love that abides in my heart? Have I developed it and practiced it?*

> **1 JOHN 4:16,17,20,21**
> **16 And we have known and BELIEVED THE LOVE THAT GOD HATH TO US. God is love; and HE THAT DWELLETH IN LOVE DWELLETH IN GOD, and God in him.**
> **17 HEREIN IS OUR LOVE MADE PERFECT** [mature], **that we may have boldness in the day of judgment: because as he is, so are we in this world. . . .**

**20 If a man say, I love God, and HATETH HIS
BROTHER, he is a liar: for he that LOVETH NOT
HIS BROTHER whom he hath seen, how can he
love God whom he hath not seen?
21 And this commandment have we from him,
That HE WHO LOVETH GOD LOVE HIS
BROTHER ALSO.**

I want you to notice verse 16: "*. . . we have known
and believed the love that God hath to us.*" The Bible is
saying that we not only believe in God, but as Christians, we believe in love. Do you believe in the God-kind
of love? Well, if you do, then practice it! Walk in it!

The love of God in your heart won't be developed
unless *you* exercise it. The love of God won't constrain
you unless *you* let it constrain you. It doesn't just work
automatically. You have a part to play in whether or not
God's love ever grows and develops in your life.

**1 JOHN 3:14,15
14 We know that we have passed from death unto
life, because we love the brethren. HE THAT
LOVETH NOT HIS BROTHER ABIDETH IN
[spiritual] DEATH.
15 WHOSOEVER HATETH HIS BROTHER IS A
MURDERER: and ye know that no murderer hath
eternal life abiding in him.**

This Scripture says that if we hate our brother — or
anyone else for that matter — we are still abiding in
spiritual death. Then verse 15 is even stronger. It says
that whoever hates his brother is a murderer. That's
strong language!

According to the Bible, you don't have to kill someone to be a murderer *in your heart*. According to that
definition, we've probably got a lot of murderers sitting
in church pews!

Then there are also those who have literally killed
people, and they have to pay for their crime. But right
on the other hand, in the sight of God, if you hate someone, God calls that being a murderer in your heart.

The Woman Who Said —
'I Hate My Mother-in-Law'

My wife and I once held a meeting in the western
part of the United States. A young couple who were in
the ministry went out to eat with us after the service.

The woman said to me, "Brother Hagin, tonight you
quoted the Scripture from First John 3:15: *'Whosoever
hateth his brother is a murderer: and ye know that no
murderer hath eternal life abiding in him.'*"

I said, "I sure did. I plead guilty." When I quoted
that verse, the Spirit of God inspired me to add, "That
means *mother-in-law* too."

She said, "But I hate my mother-in-law." Here she
was an ordained minister, and she said that she hated
her mother-in-law!

I said, "If you do, the Bible says you're a murderer,
and you don't have eternal life abiding in you. God
wouldn't tell you to love your brother — that means
mother-in-law too — if it were impossible to do so."

I knew she didn't really hate her mother-in-law, but I wanted to get her located so she could see herself in the light of God's Word. You see, just because *I* realized that she didn't really hate her mother-in-law, that wouldn't help her; I had to get *her* to see it.

Just because you see a spiritual truth, that won't help the other fellow; he's got to see it. And just because *someone else* sees a spiritual truth, that won't help you; *you* have to see it.

I knew she was saved, filled with the Holy Ghost, and she loved God. But I knew she was letting her head get in the way, and she was letting her flesh dominate her.

So I said to her, "Look me in the eye and say, 'I hate my mother-in-law,' and at the same time check down in your spirit."

The Bible didn't say that the love of God is shed abroad in our head. It said God's love is shed abroad in our heart or spirit. That's why I told her to check down in her heart.

She looked across the table and said to me, "I hate my mother-in-law."

I said, "When you said that, what happened in your spirit?"

She said, "There's something in my spirit scratching me."

I said, "I know it. That's the love of God in your spirit, trying to get your attention. The love of God is trying to constrain you so you'll love like God loves."

"What should I do?" she asked.

I said, "You're going to have to act just like you would if you loved your mother-in-law because you really do love her! The way out of the situation is to walk in love even when your flesh doesn't want to.

"Love is revealed in word and action, so you're going to have to act like you love her because you really do."

You see, walking in love means *acting* in love because the God-kind of love is not just a feeling, it's a decision and an action. You've got to demonstrate that love. You can keep the love that is shed abroad in your heart captive and shut up in your heart by giving it no expression.

Well, how do you let the love of God out of your heart so you can express it? You let it out in action. You let it out in words. It's the same way with faith because faith works by love. You can have a heart full of faith and die.

You can have a heart full of faith and never get an answer to prayer. You've got to get that faith out of your heart and into expression. You've got to get it working. How do you do that? Through actions and words. Love without expression or action will eventually dwindle and die.

It's like the ole boy who wrote a love letter to his girlfriend, saying:

I'd climb the highest mountain for you! I'd wade the deepest river! I'd swim the largest ocean just for you. And if it doesn't rain Saturday night, I'll come to see you!

No, love is revealed in word *and* action!

I told this young minister's wife, "If you really hate your mother-in-law, First John 3:15 says you are a murderer. I don't believe you are a murderer because you are born again, and you have eternal life abiding in you. That means you have the love and the life of God abiding in you. But you have to act on that love and put it to work for you before it will become a reality in your life."

This woman didn't really hate her mother-in-law. But she made the mistake so many believers make. She was listening to her head rather than to her heart.

It absolutely astounds me the way some Christian people use the word "hate." Many use the word "hate" too loosely. That word is not in my vocabulary. I don't even like to say, "I hate spinach." I may dislike some things, but I don't even hate *things*, much less *people*.

But I've even heard Christians say, "I just hate ole So-and-so." I thought to myself, *Well, then, you ought to get saved!*

I know they really don't mean that; they're just talking out of their head and letting their flesh dominate them. If they really did hate someone, then they'd be murderers in their heart, and they wouldn't have eternal life.

Of course they were saved, but they kept the love that's in their heart shut away in prison, so to speak. People who talk like that are carnal Christians who are allowing their natural mind and their flesh to dominate them. They'll need to grow up and develop in love.

No, if people are born again, they don't hate people. If they do, they don't have the life and the love of God abiding in them. If they hate people, then in their heart, they are a murderer.

When believers say they hate someone, they just need to crucify the flesh and walk according to the love of God in their spirits. That isn't always easy, and it doesn't always feel good to the flesh. In fact, it's hard on the flesh!

But that is why we need to get our minds renewed with the Word and let the love of God abide in us and be made manifest in us. We need to learn to respond to the love of God that already abides in us.

A few days later this woman invited my wife and me over to her house. She also invited her mother-in-law and her family. She came over to me and said, "You were right. I don't hate my mother-in-law. These folks are Christians, and they love God.

"I was just operating in the natural, and I let my emotions get ahold of me. I let my natural reasoning and my flesh dominate me. The love of God is in my heart. I love them. They're wonderful people and they love God."

After talking to that young couple, we learned that they were trying to believe God for their little girl's healing. Their youngest child had had epileptic seizures since she was two years old, and they had taken the child to a leading specialist.

The specialist had said, "This is the worst case of epilepsy I've seen in thirty-eight years of medical practice."

Not only that, but the child seemed to be mentally retarded, and her coordination wasn't right.

Some time later, this couple called me and asked me to come and pray for their child because she was having an epileptic attack. My wife and I got into the car to go to their house to pray, and just as real as though someone were sitting in the back seat, the Holy Spirit spoke to me.

Now I want you to listen very carefully to what I'm about to say because it can mean the difference between life and death. It can mean the difference between how long you live and whether or not you get healed.

The Holy Spirit said to me, "Don't pray for the child. Don't lay hands on the child. When you get there, say to the mother that I said, 'Under the Old Covenant, I said to Israel, "Walk in My statutes and keep My commandments, do that which is right in My sight, and I'll take sickness away from the midst of you, and the number of your days, you will fulfill."'"

Then the Holy Spirit said, "Paraphrasing that in New Testament language, I said, 'A new commandment I give you that you love one another. By this shall all men know that you are My disciples, because you have love one toward another'" (John 13:34,35).

Of course, I knew what God said under the Old Covenant in Exodus chapter 23.

EXODUS 23:25,26
25 . . . ye shall serve the Lord your God, and he
shall bless thy bread, and thy water; and I WILL

TAKE SICKNESS AWAY FROM THE MIDST OF THEE.
26 There shall nothing cast their young, nor be barren, in thy land: THE NUMBER OF THY DAYS I WILL FULFIL.

We could translate these verses in this way and do them no injustice: "Keep My commandment of love, and I will take sickness away from the midst of you, and the number of your days I will fulfill."

Then the Holy Spirit said, "Say to the mother, 'Tell Satan, "Satan, I'm walking in love now. Take your hands off of my child."'"

You see, there are times you shouldn't lay hands on people for healing. In fact, if certain conditions are not met, you could lay hands on them until you wore every hair off their head, and they wouldn't get a thing in the world out of it except a bald head.

Laying hands on people when they need to make an adjustment in their heart will only hinder their faith because nothing will happen.

We arrived at this couple's house, and I told this mother exactly what God had instructed me to say. The mother pointed to her child who was having a seizure right then, and said, "Satan, I'm walking in love now. Take your hands off my child!" As fast as you could snap your fingers, the seizure stopped, and the child was normal. Every symptom instantly left that little girl!

You see, if you're not walking in love, you won't be able to do that. The devil will laugh at you the entire time you are rebuking him. Why? Because the Bible says to give the devil no place (Eph. 4:27). If you're not walking in love, you're giving the devil a place in your life. You're opening the door to him.

But start walking in love and you will be walking in the Spirit. It doesn't take long to get in the Spirit. Just repent and ask the Lord to forgive you for not walking in love. Then determine, "From this moment on, I'm going to walk in love." Then you are in a position to put the devil in his place.

If Christians ever learned to really let the God-kind of love dominate them, you wouldn't have to anoint them with oil to get them healed. You wouldn't have to pray for them. They would get healed, and they could walk in divine health!

Where many Christians fail is that they allow unforgiveness to dominate them, and they fail to walk in love. Believers who are struggling with unforgiveness and lack of love are acting like carnal Christians.

One translation calls carnal Christians "body-ruled Christians." Baby Christians are primarily body-ruled. If you are letting your body rule you, then your natural mind is ruling you. All your natural mind knows is what it has learned through the five physical senses.

When folks understand the biblical teachings on how to practice and develop the God-kind of love, they will grow and develop beyond the babyhood stage of Christianity.

When Believers understand the benefits of walking in the God-kind of love, it will just change their lives.

Believers would have to go outside the church to find someone to pray for because everyone in the church would be healed!

Well, five years later these parents of this epileptic child visited one of our meetings in another state. By that time the child was eight years old. I asked them how their daughter was doing.

This couple told me, "She's been in perfect health. In fact, she had the highest IQ of anyone in her school."

I asked them, "In this five-year period, has she ever had any other symptoms?"

The mother said, "Twice there were some little symptoms that showed up."

"What did you do?" I asked.

She said, "I just said, 'Oh, no you don't, Satan! I'm walking in love now.' And our daughter was all right."

That happened many years ago now, but then in 1991 these parents came to our annual Campmeeting. Of course, their daughter was a grown woman by then.

My wife and I talked to them and asked them how their daughter was doing. They said, "From that time to this, she's never had another seizure."

Someone said, "Oh, I wish I could get that to work for me." You don't get it to work by wishing. It works by walking in love — by *acting* on the God-kind of love. You've got to act on the Word of God and exercise the God-kind of love because faith works by love.

Someone said, "But I haven't always walked in love." That woman hadn't either. But the minute she repented and began walking in love, she had a right to claim God's promises.

The problem with most folks is that they dwell on the past. They focus on what they've done wrong, rather than on the mercy and forgiveness of God.

For example, they say, "But I did this and I did that. I just don't deserve God's forgiveness." You can't dwell on those areas where you've missed it. Just repent. Take God at His Word. God said, *"If we confess our sins, he is faithful and just to forgive us our sins, and to cleanse us from ALL unrighteousness"* (1 John 1:9). How much of our unrighteousness? *All* of it!

And if you know you are walking in love and Satan attacks you, your children, or your home, you can boldly say, "Satan, take your hands off my children because I'm walking in love. Satan, take your hands off me and off my home because I'm walking in love!"

And if you get out of the love walk, run as fast as you can and get back under the protective umbrella of love. The New Covenant belongs to you, so walk in love so you can prosper in every area of life. Walking in love will work for you just as much as it will for anyone. So learn to walk in love and reap the benefits that God's love brings.

'I'll Take Sickness From the Midst of You'

When the Holy Spirit spoke those Scriptures to me in Exodus 23:25,26, it came as a real revelation to me. I had never seen those Scriptures in exactly that light.

But the truth is, that promise belongs to us under the New Covenant, too, for the simple reason that we have a better covenant established on better promises. If something is better, it includes all that the old one had plus more, or it wouldn't be better.

HEBREWS 8:6
6   But now hath he obtained A MORE EXCEL-LENT MINISTRY, by how much also he is THE MEDIATOR OF A BETTER COVENANT, which was ESTABLISHED UPON BETTER PROMISES.

The Israelites had the promise that if they walked in obedience to God, He would take sickness from them and fulfill their days. If they had that promise under the Old Covenant, then it stands to reason that we can also claim that promise because we are under a better covenant than they were.

Think about it. Under the Old Covenant, by keeping God's commandments and His statutes and doing what He said, the Israelites had the potential of living their full length of time out here on earth without sickness.

Well, if that promise is not for us under the New Covenant, then that would mean we *lost* benefits when Jesus came, died on the Cross, and ratified a new and better covenant.

But that's not what the Bible says! It doesn't say that we have a *worse* covenant established on *inferior* promises! No, it says we have a *better* covenant, which was established upon *better* promises.

What would you think if you heard someone talking to another person, saying, "I heard you bought a house".

The person answered, "Yes, we used to live in a brand-new home with four bedrooms, wall-to-wall carpeting, and three baths. But now we live in an old house with one bedroom and a half bath. Oh, it's just so much *better*."

If someone said that, you'd think there was something wrong with him, wouldn't you? If something is better, it includes what the old one had plus more besides, or else it wouldn't be better.

In other words, God took sickness away from Israel for walking in His laws. Well, since we are under a new and better covenant, does that mean that since Jesus came, we have to go through life sick and afflicted? If that's true, it would have been better if He hadn't come! Of course that's ridiculous.

Does it make any sense that we can fulfill the Law by walking in love — but we have to stay sick! No, that would be foolish, wouldn't it?

Not only that, but this promise in Exodus 15:26 was given to the Israelites who were not *sons* of God; they were *servants* of God. Well, if it wasn't God's will that His *servants* be sick, then how could it be His will for His *sons* to be sick (Lev. 25:55; 1 John 3:2)?

I don't know about you, but I want God's best. Years ago, I saw the benefits of walking in love, and I determined in my heart that I'm going to walk in love whether anyone else does or not!

EXODUS 15:26
26 . . . If thou wilt diligently hearken to the voice
of the Lord thy God, and wilt do that which is
right in his sight, and wilt give ear to his commandments, and keep all his statutes, I will put
[permit] **none of these diseases upon thee, which I
have brought upon the Egyptians: for I AM THE
LORD THAT HEALETH THEE.**

If you read this verse in the *King James* translation,
you will get the impression that God literally puts diseases on people. But some of these Hebrew verbs should
have been translated in the *permissive* sense, not in the
causative sense.

In other words, we know by studying the entire
Bible that sickness and disease don't come from
Heaven. God does not *cause* sickness and disease, nor
does He afflict anyone with sickness or disease.

Besides, even from reading this verse in Exodus 15,
we can clearly see that sickness wasn't the will of God
for the Israelites. God wanted His people well. That's
why He told them, "I am the Lord that *healeth* thee."

Well, someone could say, "But in Exodus 15:26, it
says God puts sickness on people." If you think God is
the one putting sickness on people, you need to do some
studying and digging in the Word.

Let me give you this illustration to show you what I
mean. In the days of the gold rush, people discovered
gold out in California. Well, you could pan a little gold
dust out of a river, and once in a while, you could even
find a nugget. But if you really wanted to strike it rich,
you had to dig for it.

It's the same way with the Bible. You can skim along the surface of the Bible and pan a little gold — some spiritual truth. You may even find a nugget here and there. But if you really want to strike it rich in the depth of the Word, you've got to dig for it.

Actually, Exodus 15:26 would have been more accurately translated like this: "If you will diligently hearken to the Voice of the Lord your God, and will do that which is right in His sight . . . I will not *permit* or *allow* these diseases to come upon you. . . ."

Several passages in the Old Testament should have been translated into English in the permissive sense instead of the causative.

For example, Isaiah 45:7 says, *"I form the light, and create darkness: I make peace, and create evil: I the Lord do all these things."* Well, when we read that verse in context with the whole Bible, it isn't consistent with the rest of the Scriptures to interpret it that God Himself *creates* evil.

Does God create evil? No, that would make God a devil. God may permit evil when people violate His Word, but He does not *create* evil. If God created evil, that would make Him the author of evil. But we know God is not the author of evil.

The New Testament tells us who is the author of evil: *"The thief cometh not, but for to steal, and to kill, and to destroy: I am come that they might have life, and that they might have it more abundantly"* (John 10:10). Satan is the thief, not God.

When you understand Isaiah 45:7 in the permissive sense, then you understand that evil is *allowed* when people get out of God's will.

For example, suppose on your way home from work today, you stopped and robbed a filling station. God would allow you to do that, wouldn't He? He wouldn't *want* you to do it because it's not His will. He certainly wouldn't *commission* you to do it. In fact, if you'd listen to Him, He'd try to keep you from doing it. But you still have free will and you *could* do it.

God does not *commission* wrongdoing. It's not His will that you to do things that are wrong. But you have free choice, and He will *allow* you to do what is wrong if you persist and continue to choose what is wrong.

Suppose you had a four-year-old child, and you were cooking on the stove in a cast-iron skillet. You saw that your child was about to put his hand on that hot skillet, so you said to him, "Honey, don't do that. It will burn you!"

All of a sudden, your child sticks his hand out and puts it on the hot skillet anyway. You didn't *commission* your child to do that. But you did *allow* it in the sense that your child has free will, and even though you warned him, he could still put his hand on the hot burner.

You told him not to do it, and you even warned him of the consequences. But the child persisted and touched the hot skillet anyway.

Did you allow it in the sense of commissioning it? No, of course not. You only allowed it in the sense that the child had free choice, and he could choose to disobey you. You see, man has free choice. God wants to bless him, but when he disobeys, he causes the hand of God's blessing to lift from him.

That's what happened to the Israelites. God had to allow or *permit* sickness and disease when the Israelites sinned and disobeyed Him.

That's what God was saying: "If you don't keep My commandments, these things are going to come upon you. However, it's not My will that they come upon you. If you'll walk in My statutes, none of these things will happen to you."

Also look at the Book of Amos.

AMOS 3:6
6   Shall a trumpet be blown in the city, and the people not be afraid? shall there be evil in a city, and the Lord hath not done it?

You can interpret this Scripture in several different ways. It says, " . . . *shall there be evil in a city . . . ?*" Well, I wonder if there was any evil done last night in the city where you live? Of course there was. Did the Lord do it? No, He didn't do it. You see, if God commits evil, then He has no right whatsoever to judge man for sinning or committing evil.

God does not commit or create evil. He only permits it in the sense that people have free will and they can disobey Him and get out from under His protective hand of blessing. There is a vast difference between commission and permission.

It's just like the example of the child and the hot burner. You didn't commission that little child to touch the hot skillet. But you permitted it only in the sense that the child has free will and could chose to touch the skillet even though you told him not to.

Dr. Robert E. Young, author of *Young's Hebrew and Greek Concordance*, was an outstanding Hebrew scholar. He points out that the translators had no permissive sense for the verbs, so the scholars translated these verbs into the causative tense instead of the permissive tense.

For example, this verse in Amos 3:6 should have been translated into the permissive tense, not the causative tense: "If there is evil in the city, the Lord permitted it." God may permit evil in the sense that people have free choice and they can choose to do evil, but He does not cause it, nor does He condone it.

Another verse along this line that has been much discussed is found in First Samuel chapter 16.

1 SAMUEL 16:14
14 But the Spirit of the Lord departed from Saul, and an evil spirit from the Lord troubled him.

Because the English has no corresponding permissive tense to these Hebrew words, these verbs were translated into the causative tense. This is misleading, because it makes it sound like God is causing and creating evil and even sending evil spirits to people.

No, God does not send evil spirits to people. God will permit these things to come upon people because of their wrongdoing and disobedience. Actually, when they disobey, people get themselves out from under His protective hand of blessing — but it isn't God's will or desire that evil comes against them. God is not the agent who puts sickness or disease on people.

For example, when King Saul backslid, did God take the Holy Spirit away from him? And did God commission that evil spirit to go trouble Saul? No, because that doesn't fit with the rest of the doctrine of the Bible.

No, demons and evil spirits don't come from God. What actually happened was that when Saul sinned, he broke fellowship with God. That allowed the devil an inroad into Saul's life. God didn't commission it, but He permitted that evil spirit from the devil to trouble Saul.

Actually, Saul's own disobedience allowed the evil spirit access into his life.

The original Hebrew for these Scriptures was in the permissive sense. But because the English translation had no corresponding permissive sense at the time, the verbs were translated into the causative. That has caused misunderstanding in Bible interpretation since then.

No, God does not send plagues and sickness upon people as certain translations would seem to indicate. God does not put sickness upon His people, for the simple reason that God's Word teaches us that sickness comes from Satan (John 10:10; Acts 10:38).

Besides, God doesn't have any sickness; there isn't any sickness in Heaven. Therefore, if God puts sickness on people, He'd have to steal it from Satan. But God is not a thief. No, God is not the one who puts sickness on people. Satan does that.

Not only that, but you have to interpret Scripture in the light of other Scripture. As you read through the Bible, you find that the Bible is progressive revelation. You don't get the full revelation of anything in the Old Testament. But when you come into the New Testament, then you begin to get the full revelation of the Word.

God's Word does *not* teach that evil, sickness, and disease come from God. But rather, when God's people break His commandments, they get out from under His divine protection. *They* open the door to the devil themselves and allow Satan to bring these afflictions upon them by their own disobedience.

ACTS 10:38
38 How God anointed Jesus of Nazareth with the Holy Ghost and with power: who went about doing good, and healing all that were OPPRESSED OF THE DEVIL; for God was with him.

You can see that in the New Testament, sickness is called *satanic* oppression, not *divine* oppression. If God put sickness on people, it would have to be *divine* oppression.

No, these folks were oppressed of the *devil*. Therefore, when you're dealing with sickness, you're dealing with Satan because Satan and sickness are synonymous terms.

The Bible says that Jesus was manifested to destroy the works of the devil. Among the works that Jesus destroyed were sickness and disease. Israel's sin and wrongdoing brought these dreadful plagues and sicknesses upon them. The same thing happens today.

God doesn't want sickness to come on us, but if we're not going to walk in His ways, then we open a door to the devil, and sickness and disease can come on us. That's why under the New Covenant, Jesus gave us a new commandment of love. When we're fulfilling the New Testament commandment of love, Satan doesn't have an inroad into our lives.

'The Number of Your Days I Will Fulfill'

Under the Old Testament, the Israelites broke God's commandments, and when they did, they took themselves out from under God's divine protection. They couldn't claim His protection and blessing anymore, so they were actually the ones who permitted Satan access into their lives.

Because of their disobedience, God had to permit sickness, disease, or evil to come upon them unless they repented, because they had opened a door to the devil themselves.

Their own sin and wrongdoing were what brought those dreadful diseases and plagues upon Israel. God had promised, "If you'll keep My commandments, I'll take sickness away from the midst of thee, for I am the Lord that healeth thee." As long as the Israelites kept God's statutes and commandments, they never needed to be sick.

If God would take sickness from the midst of them under the Old Covenant, which is not as good a covenant as ours, how much more will He do that for us under the New Covenant? Under the new and better covenant, it does *not* say, "Keep the New Covenant law of love, and you'll be sick and afflicted all your life."

Paraphrasing the New Covenant law of love, you could read Exodus 15:26 and Exodus 23:25,26 like this: "Walk in My commandment of love and keep My precepts of love; do that which is right in My sight by walking in love; and I'll take sickness away from the midst of you, and the number of your days, I shall fulfill."

Under the New Covenant, Romans 13:8 says, "*. . . for he that loveth another hath fulfilled the law.*" If we fulfill the Law by fulfilling the New Covenant commandment that Jesus gave us — to love one another — then we can claim the same promise the Israelites could claim.

It doesn't make any sense to say that if we fulfill the New Covenant law of love, we would get a curse rather than a blessing. That isn't scriptural.

Deuteronomy 28 lists the curses for breaking the law of God. These curses include eleven different diseases. The curse of the Law also lists "every disease and every sickness that is not written in the book of this Law" (Deut. 28:61).

You can readily see from reading Deuteronomy 28 that sickness is a curse of the Law. It is a curse that comes on mankind because of breaking God's commandments.

But under the New Covenant, Jesus redeemed us from the curse of the Law (Gal. 3:13). Jesus came to heal the sick and afflicted! Jesus said in John 10:10: *". . . I am come that they might have life, and that they might have it more abundantly."*

We didn't *lose* benefits when Jesus came to this earth and died for the sins of mankind! We *gained* blessings and benefits because Jesus came to give us life and that more abundantly.

> **EXODUS 23:25,26**
> **25 And ye shall serve the Lord your God, and he shall bless thy bread, and thy water; and I WILL TAKE SICKNESS AWAY FROM THE MIDST OF THEE.**
> **26 There shall nothing cast their young, nor be barren, in thy land: THE NUMBER OF THY DAYS I WILL FULFIL.**

What does that Scripture mean, *" . . . the number of thy days I will fulfil"*? God didn't promise the Israelites that they wouldn't die. He said they would fulfill the number of their days.

What is the number of our days? In Psalm 91:16, David was quoting the Lord when he said, *"With long life will I satisfy him, and shew him my salvation."*

What is long life? Psalm 90:10 says, *"The days of our years are threescore years and ten* [70 years]*; and if by reason of strength they be fourscore years* [80 years]*. . . ."*

When you get to be 70 years old, if you're not satisfied, go on to 80 years. Just live until you get satisfied!

And when you're 80 years old, if you're not satisfied, then hang around awhile longer.

Enjoying a long life full of good days is up to us more than we realize. You remember what Paul said writing to the Philippians:

> **PHILIPPIANS 1:21-24**
> **21 For to me to live is Christ, and to die is gain.**
> **22 But if I live in the flesh, this is the fruit of my labour: yet what I shall choose I wot not.**
> **23 For I am in a strait betwixt two, having a desire to depart, and to be with Christ; which is far better:**
> **24 Nevertheless to abide in the flesh is more needful for you.**

In other words, Paul was saying that living on in the flesh was more needful for the Church because then he could teach and minister to them. But he was saying, "I don't know whether I'm going to choose to stay here or go to be with Christ, which is far better."

How To Prolong Your Life

You hear people say, "It's not up to us when we die. It's all up to God." No, it isn't all up to God. God put certain laws into motion, and He gave us His Word. Now to a large extent, it's up to us.

Go back and read the Psalms and the Proverbs. Notice how many times these Books of the Bible talk about people doing certain things that weren't right, and it says, "Their days will be shortened" (Ps. 89:45; 102:23; Prov. 10:27).

Other Scriptures say that doing certain things will *add* to your life and give you length of days (Prov. 3:16). So to a certain extent, it's up to people whether their days are lengthened or shortened.

DEUTERONOMY 4:40
40 Thou shalt keep therefore his statutes, and his commandments, which I command thee this day, that it may go well with thee, and WITH THY CHILDREN AFTER THEE, and THAT THOU MAYEST PROLONG THY DAYS UPON THE EARTH, which the Lord thy God giveth thee, for ever.

This Scripture doesn't say, "Keep My commandments so you can live a short time upon the earth." No, God is trying to tell us how we can *prolong* our days.

What does it mean to prolong your days? It means to live longer on this earth. And this Scripture says that even your children will be blessed.

In other words, by doing what God said, we will prolong our days and live longer on the earth. That doesn't mean we won't die, but it means that if we obey the Lord, we can live a long, good life. Well, under the New Covenant, the commandment God has given us to obey is the law of love.

As I said, there are a number of statements in the Book of Proverbs that tell us how to shorten our days or to prolong them.

PROVERBS 3:16
16 LENGTH OF DAYS [long life] **IS IN HER** [wisdom's] **RIGHT HAND; and in her left hand riches and honour.**

PROVERBS 9:11
11 For by me [wisdom of God's Word] **THY DAYS SHALL BE MULTIPLIED, and THE YEARS OF THY LIFE SHALL BE INCREASED.**

PROVERBS 10:27
27 THE FEAR OF THE LORD PROLONGETH DAYS: but the years of the wicked shall be shortened.

PROVERBS 28:16
16 The prince that wanteth understanding is also a great oppressor: but he that hateth covetousness SHALL PROLONG HIS DAYS.

You see, God made provision for us to prolong our days. Now it's up to us to walk in the light of His provision. How do we do that? By walking in love toward others! Study the Bible for yourself on the subject of love. You'll find out just how much the Bible has to say about love and health and living a long time on the earth.

In fact, I am convinced that if the Body of Christ really walked in the love of God, they wouldn't need *healing*; they could walk in divine *health*.

But just by virtue of the fact that the Bible has so much to say about the subject of God's love, you can see that it is important for the Body of Christ to find out more about this subject.

When I was a young minister, I heard an older minister who had been in the ministry for more than fifty years say something that has served me well over the years.

He said, "Anytime you find some Scripture or a biblical subject that's only mentioned once in the entire Bible, you know it's not of major importance."

There's a lot of truth to that statement. Did you ever stop to think about that? Well, the Bible does say, ". . . *In the mouth of two or three witnesses shall every word be established*" (2 Cor. 13:1). How many witnesses? Two or three.

Therefore, if a Bible subject is of great importance, it would be mentioned over and over again in the Word. And yet sometimes people are prone to take one little Scripture and run off with it and try to build a major doctrine on it. That's foolish.

Just think how many times the subject of love is mentioned in one way or another in the Bible. The New Testament writers wrote about this subject over and over again.

If you want to know about a Bible subject, find other Scriptures in the New Testament that confirm the same thing or the same subject. We're not as concerned about the Old Testament, because we're not under the Old Covenant. In fact, you can't be a successful Christian by just dwelling in the Old Testament.

For example, some people teach that we don't have any promises in this life. They say, "Oh, we can be saved all right and born again, but down here on this earth, all we can hope for is to wander like a beggar through the heat and the cold. It'll all be over soon, but we've got no promises we can rely on."

One minister even said, "Long life is not a New Testament promise. It was just a promise to Israel."

Don't accept something just because some preacher said it! When I was a teenager, I trained myself that no matter what anyone said or did, I would first of all ask myself, *What does the Word of God say about it?*

Well, no one would dispute that long life was a promise to Israel, all right. But when this minister said long life is not a New Testament promise, I thought to myself, *Well, I always thought the Book of Ephesians was in the New Testament!*

> **EPHESIANS 6:1-3**
> **1   Children, obey your parents in the Lord: for this is right.**
> **2   Honour thy father and mother; WHICH IS THE FIRST COMMANDMENT WITH PROMISE;**
> **3   That IT MAY BE WELL WITH THEE, and THOU MAYEST LIVE LONG ON THE EARTH.**

Paul said that children who obey their parents would live a long time — where? On the earth. So this passage is talking about our natural life here on this earth.

Did Paul say to obey your parents so you could live a *short* time on the earth? No, he said that when you obey your parents, you'll not only live a long time on the earth, but it will be well with you.

Well, if you were walking in the God-kind of love, would you honor your parents? Of course you would. When you honor your parents, you are walking in love. That's why, whatever situation arises, always ask yourself, *What would love do?*

In this Scripture, "Honour thy father and mother," Paul is quoting from the Old Testament Ten Commandments.

EXODUS 20:12
12 Honour thy father and thy mother: THAT THY DAYS MAY BE LONG UPON THE LAND which the Lord thy God giveth thee.

Someone said, "I thought you said we weren't supposed to keep the Ten Commandments." No, that's not what I said. I said that if we walk in love, we automatically fulfill *all* of the Ten Commandments.

Obeying your parents is the first one of the Ten Commandments that contains a promise. This is God's promise to you if you honor your father and your mother: "That it may be *well* with you and you may live a *long* time on the earth."

Don't you know that if children walk in divine love toward their parents, they're going to obey them. Children who walk in obedience to their parents become recipients of the promise of long life because they're fulfilling this commandment by keeping the New Testament law of love.

But some people seem to think God's Word is going to work for them whether or not they are living right or walking in love. But it won't. All the faith confessions in the world won't work if you're not living right.

Parents: Walk in Love Toward Your Children

But there is another side to this too. If children have to walk in love toward their parents so they can live long on the earth, parents also have the responsibility to walk in love toward their children.

I don't know about you, but as our children were growing up, I sometimes had to ask them to forgive me. I would say to them, "I was right in correcting you, but wrong in the way I did it. I want you to forgive me." It makes all the difference in the world when you raise your children with the love of God in your heart!

If parents will walk in love toward their children and live right before them, it will affect their children spiritually, mentally, and physically. It will even affect their health.

I don't know about you, but I have strong feelings in many of these areas. I don't know whether I get mad myself or whether it's just my righteous indignation that gets stirred up. But people who are leaving their families and abandoning their children need to know that they are going to pay for all of that one of these days. Not only that, but if only people knew the effect it has on children when they're abandoned by a parent!

When I was holding a meeting in California several years ago, I happened to pick up a newspaper and read that researchers had done a survey in the California penitentiaries. They found out that without exception every single person who was in prison for a violent crime had been abused as a child. Every single one of them!

That doesn't mean parents shouldn't discipline their children. Of course they have to discipline their children. Even when you're walking in love toward your children, you still have to reprimand them from time to time, because children are children. And at times you've got to spank them. And sometimes it seems like boys need more discipline than girls!

But, for instance, I never spanked Ken without reading the Word to him first. If you spank your children in anger, you're wrong because you're not walking in love toward them.

Before I'd spank Ken, I'd open the Bible to this passage in Ephesians. I'd say, "Son, I'm not spanking you because I want to or because I want to be mean to you. But I want you to stay well; I want you to live a long time on the earth." Then I'd read him Ephesians 6:1-3.

My wife and I read the Word and prayed with our children every night before they went to bed. And when they started school, we'd read the Word and pray with them before they went to school every morning.

Well, both our children grew up serving God and are now ordained ministers. But we lived right in front of them too. All the faith confessions in the world wouldn't have done any good if we hadn't walked in love toward them and lived right in front of them.

As parents, sometimes you have to reprimand your children, because the Bible says that a child left to himself brings a reproach to his parents (Prov. 29:15). But you can still walk in divine love and discipline your children.

I remember when Ken was about six years old, he came into my study one night when I was praying. He said, "Daddy, I want you to forgive me."

I said, "What for, son?"

"Well," he said, "you told me to empty that wastebasket this morning, and I didn't do it. Read that Scripture to me about where it says it will be well with you, and you don't have to be sick, and you can live a long time on the earth."

So I read Ephesians 6:1-3 to him. Then I said, "I forgive you, son. Now let's just kneel down here and ask the Lord to forgive you."

There is a promise that goes along with honoring your parents and walking in love with them — and it's a long, good life!

As we all know, you can know about a Bible subject, but if you don't put into practice what you know, it won't profit you. It's the principles of love applied that brings forth fruit.

The God-kind of love is important in every area of your life. Walking in love affects every area of your life, including how long you live on the earth. Begin to put the love of God to practice, and watch God's love bring forth great fruit.

Chapter 7
Judge Yourself —
And You Won't Be Judged

When God gave us the New Testament law of love, He said we are to love our neighbor as we love ourselves. That just means we are to love our fellow man and our fellow believer as we would love ourselves. The Bible also said, *"As we have therefore opportunity, let us do good unto all men, especially unto them who are of the household of faith"* (Gal. 6:10).

Well, we don't need to look around and judge the other fellow and see if he's walking in love. We just need to be sure *we* are doing right and that *we* are walking in love ourselves! If we judge others, it will just cause strife and discord in the Body of Christ.

Notice what Galatians 5:15 says about strife and discord.

GALATIANS 5:15
15 But if ye bite and devour one another, take heed that ye be not consumed one of another.

Biting and devouring one another is not walking in love. The reason some people are sick a lot and even die prematurely is that they don't walk in love. There is a consequence for sowing strife and discord and for judging others.

GALATIANS 6:7
7 Be not deceived; God is not mocked: for WHAT-SOEVER A MAN SOWETH, THAT SHALL HE ALSO REAP.

Normally, when we read this verse, we think about the sinner who is out drinking, cussing, and running around. But did you ever stop to think about it? This verse wasn't even written to sinners. It was written to Christians. God was talking to believers when He said, "Whatever a man sows, he will reap." As a believer, if you don't act in love, you will reap that too.

There is a truth in this verse that applies to sinners, of course. Some people preach this verse to sinners, but actually, when Paul wrote this, he was talking to the believers at Galatia and to Christians everywhere.

He was saying that Christians need to wake up and understand that even though God is a loving God, He will not be mocked. Whatsoever a man sows, that is what he *will* reap! In other words, sooner or later, his chickens will come home to roost. His sins will find him out (Num. 32:23).

I've been in the ministry for nearly sixty-five years, and I've found out that if you just keep on walking in love, in the process of time, some of those folks who judged you and did you wrong will be the very ones who come back to you for help. Very often God sends them back. And, thank God, because you're walking in love, you can help them.

But this Scripture in Galatians 6:7 also has another application.

When you act in love, you're going to reap a reward for that too! What are you going to reap for walking in love? Health, healing, long life, and prosperity!

You see, if you keep feeding the love nature that's in you with the Word and you keep practicing it, the God-kind of love will grow and develop in your life. And by putting the God-kind of love into practice by acting on it, you will reap the benefits and the results of walking in love.

I don't know about you, but I'm going to sow love! And if I sow God's love, then I will reap the results that love brings because I've fulfilled the Law. Then sickness will be taken away from the midst of me, and the number of my days God will fulfill.

Discern the Lord's Body

What we've got to realize is that under the New Covenant, whether or not we fulfill the number of our days is to a large extent up to us. Why? Because healing was provided for our bodies in the atonement. The Bible says, " . . . *Himself took our infirmities, and bare our sicknesses*" (Matt. 8:17).

When Jesus said this, He was quoting from Isaiah 53:4: *"Surely he hath borne our griefs, and carried our sorrows."*

The literal Hebrew says, "He bore our *sickness* and carried our *pains*."

Then First Peter 2:24 also talks about our covenant of healing.

> **1 PETER 2:24**
> **24 Who his own self bare our sins in his own body on the tree, that we, being dead to sins, should live unto righteousness: BY WHOSE STRIPES YE WERE HEALED.**

So healing belongs to us. But we'll never be able to walk in God's provision of healing unless we learn to walk in love.

Well, if God has made healing available to us in the Atonement, then why isn't everyone healed? If we are going to walk in health, there is something we need to understand about walking in love. Notice what the Bible says in First Corinthians 11.

> **1 CORINTHIANS 11:23-30**
> **23 For I have received of the Lord that which also I delivered unto you, That the Lord Jesus the same night in which he was betrayed took bread:**
> **24 And when he had given thanks, he brake it, and said, Take, eat: this is my body, which is broken for you: this do in remembrance of me.**
> **25 After the same manner also he took the cup, when he had supped, saying, This cup is the new testament in my blood: this do ye, as oft as ye drink it, in remembrance of me.**
> **26 For as often as ye eat this bread, and drink this cup, ye do shew the Lord's death till he come.**

27 Wherefore WHOSOEVER SHALL EAT THIS BREAD, AND DRINK THIS CUP OF THE LORD, UNWORTHILY, shall be guilty of the body and blood of the Lord.
28 But LET A MAN EXAMINE HIMSELF, and so let him eat of that bread, and drink of that cup.
29 For he that eateth and drinketh UNWORTHILY, eateth and drinketh damnation to himself, NOT DISCERNING THE LORD'S BODY.
30 FOR THIS CAUSE many are WEAK and SICKLY among you, and MANY SLEEP.

Now let's go back and analyze what we just read. When Jesus took the bread, He said, "This is My Body, which is broken for you." You see, with Jesus' stripes we were healed. Because His body was broken for us in the Atonement, we can receive physical healing for our bodies.

Then Jesus said, "This cup is the New Testament in My blood." The Bible says that without the shedding of blood, there is no remission of sins (Heb. 9:22). Jesus' blood signifies our redemption and the cleansing of our sins. So in this passage of Scripture, we can see both healing for our bodies and the remission of our sins.

Then notice the word "unworthily" in verse 27: *"Wherefore whosoever shall eat this bread, and drink this cup of the Lord, unworthily, shall be guilty of the body and blood of the Lord."*

The word used here is not "unworthy." Many times folks say, "I feel so unworthy," and they think this verse applies to feelings of unworthiness. But verse 27 is *not* saying that we are unworthy to partake of the Lord's Supper.

The word "unworthily" refers to *the manner and attitude* in which you partake of the Lord's Supper. So this verse is talking about the manner in which the Corinthians were partaking of the Lord's Supper.

If you'll read the previous verses and study the context, you'll see that these folks were coming together, having a meal, and also taking the Lord's Supper. But some of them even drank wine and got drunk. So Paul was saying, "These folks are bringing condemnation or judgment on themselves because they are partaking of the Lord's Supper in an unworthy manner."

Then the Bible goes on to say, "For this cause many are weak and sickly and many sleep or die prematurely." That infers that we should not be weak or sickly. Paul is talking about man's physical body here. He's saying that those who partake of the Lord's Supper in an unworthy manner can become weak and sickly and even die prematurely.

These verses are saying, "By not discerning the Lord's body, many are weak and sickly among you and many sleep." By "sleep" the Bible means that their bodies are asleep in the grave, and their spirits have gone to be with the Lord.

But notice that they died *prematurely*. The number of their days were *not* fulfilled. They shouldn't have died. It certainly wasn't God's will that they die prematurely. Actually, if they had discerned the Lord's body, they wouldn't have been weak and sickly, and they wouldn't have died prematurely.

The Bible is saying that sometimes there is a *cause* or a reason some people are weak, sickly, and even die prematurely, because if they don't discern the Lord's body, they bring judgment on themselves.

Did you notice that it didn't say anything about not discerning the Lord's blood. It said, "Not discerning the Lord's *body*." To "discern" means *to see and understand.*

The breaking of the Communion bread is a symbol or type of the broken body of Jesus. If you don't see and understand that Jesus' body was broken for your physical sustenance and healing, then even though you may be walking in love, you can go right on being weak and sickly by not appropriating the healing that was already provided for you on the Cross of Calvary.

Christ is our Passover Lamb. His body was broken for our physical sustenance and healing: *"by whose stripes ye were healed"* (1 Peter 2:24). If you don't know that you are healed by His stripes, then you can go right on being weak and sickly physically. You may even die prematurely and not live out your full length of time down here.

But there's also another side to this statement, "not discerning the Lord's body." You can also be weak, sickly, and die prematurely if you do not discern and understand that the Lord's spiritual Body, the Body of Christ, is one (Col. 3:15).

In other words, there is a spiritual Body of Christ on the earth today, which includes all the born-again believers worldwide (Col. 1:18). When Jesus was here on the earth, the only Body of Christ that was on the earth was Jesus' physical body. But today the Body of Christ consists of believers all over the world. And we need to discern the Body of Christ and walk in love toward them.

In other words, by not discerning the Body of Christ — our brothers and sisters in Christ — and walking in love toward them, we can open ourselves up to weakness, sickness, and even premature death. And the reason many believers are in a weak and sickly condition is that they have not discerned the Body of Christ as they should have.

If you do not walk in love toward fellow members of the Body of Christ, you're going to be weak and sickly, and you'll not prolong your days on this earth. You'll shorten your days, and you can even die prematurely. *I* didn't say that — the Bible said that!

Some Christians have already died prematurely because they didn't walk in love toward fellow members of the Body of Christ. They shouldn't have died — it wasn't God's best for them — but their lack of love shortened their own days.

Not walking in love can shorten your life because it allows the devil a foothold in your life. Every step out of love is a step in sin. Sin opens the door to the devil in your life. Therefore, to fulfill your days on this earth, you're going to have to walk in love.

And God's love never fails. It's God's love at work in us that will enable us to walk in love toward every member of the Body of Christ. That's because love — God's divine love in us — can settle any quarrel or any dispute. It can solve any problem because God is love. I've seen God's love work in some impossible situations over the years.

Christians may not all agree on every little bitty thing. But one thing we will all agree on is that the Word of God is true. And we will all agree that Jesus Christ is Lord and that without the shedding of His blood, there is no remission of sins.

Whether folks agree with you or not on every doctrinal issue, you can still walk in love toward them even if they don't walk in love with you. Walking in love is of the utmost importance.

Failure To Judge Yourself Results in the Lord's Judgment

Let me show you how important it is to walk in love toward those in the Body of Christ.

From 1947 through 1958, there was a healing revival here in America. There were about 120 of us in the healing ministry who belonged to an organization of evangelists called *The Voice of Healing*. We held conventions, and Gordon Lindsay published many of the healing testimonies in his magazine, *The Voice of Healing*.

Brother Oral Roberts started coming to the forefront in ministry about 1948, and eventually he got a tent that would seat 20,000 people. There was one fellow in *The Voice of Healing* who got a larger tent than Roberts' tent. He put another section in it so he could seat 22,000 and occasionally he'd fill it up.

This other fellow was also one of the leading healing evangelists in the days of *The Voice of Healing*. No one had a greater healing ministry at that time than he did.

I saw some of the greatest miracles in this evangelist's ministry that I've ever seen.

But the Lord told me, "You go tell him that he's not going to live much longer unless he judges himself." The man was only thirty-five years old at the time.

The Lord said to me, "The number-one thing he's to judge himself on is walking in love toward his fellow minister. Secondly, he needs to judge himself on money."

The Lord said the third thing this evangelist needed to judge himself on was diet. I don't mean to be unkind about it, but this man was as big as a cow and ate like a horse.

Well, we don't have to become health-food nuts. That's not what the Lord was saying. But on the other hand, I remember something John Wesley said. He said, "I don't live to eat; I just eat to live."

Was it scriptural for this minister to judge himself? Of course it was. The Lord was trying to warn him, because if he would have judged himself, the Lord wouldn't have had to judge him. That's what the Bible says.

> **1 CORINTHIANS 11:31,32**
> **31 For IF WE WOULD JUDGE OURSELVES, WE SHOULD NOT BE JUDGED.**
> **32 But WHEN WE ARE JUDGED, WE ARE CHAS-TENED OF THE LORD,** that we should not be condemned with the world.

I remember one time my wife and I were on our way to hold a meeting, and we stopped by to visit this fellow's tent meeting. In the city where he was holding this meeting, there was a state institution for deaf and mute people.

They brought five men from that institute who were totally deaf and mute to this healing evangelist's service, and he laid hands on them. Just like you'd snap your fingers, all five of them were instantly healed. They were healed in front of thousands of people.

This evangelist stopped the service right then and started taking up an offering. Then he announced to the audience, "Don't come down here unless you've got at least $50 to give in the offering."

People were running over one another to get down there to give in the offering! Now you've got to understand that this was back in the early '50s. Money was worth a lot more back then than it is now in these days of inflation. But, you see, you can't take the things of God and use them to raise money.

And sooner or later, if people don't judge themselves, these things are going to catch up with them.

Remember what the Bible says, *"Be not deceived; God is not mocked: for whatsoever a man soweth, that shall he also reap"* (Gal. 6:7). That applies to every area of people's lives.

I saw another miraculous healing in this man's ministry that was confirmed by medical science. A woman came to one of his meetings on a stretcher. Her body was as stiff as a board, just like it was petrified.

It was a very rare disease, and medical science couldn't do anything about it. If you touched her body, it felt like you just touched a piece of petrified lumber.

They brought her into the service, and when this minister laid hands on her, she was instantly healed. This minister had a marvelous healing ministry. Blind people were instantly healed. Yet the Lord said to me, "You go tell him that he's not going to live much longer unless he judges himself."

I went to talk to this healing evangelist, but he was busy talking to someone else at the time. By the time he finished talking to the other person, my natural mind had taken over, and I thought, *He doesn't walk in love toward the brethren. If I tell him what the Lord told me, he's liable to slap my face.* By then the evangelist had left, and I never had another opportunity to talk to him.

Three years later my wife and I were in Los Angeles in Angelus Temple at a *Voice of Healing* convention. In those days, we had a *Voice of Healing* convention every year at Thanksgiving time. This man's wife called the convention for prayer because the doctors said that this evangelist was dying. He was only thirty-eight years old.

Brother Lindsay announced this from the platform. He said it would hurt the healing ministry if this foremost healing minister in America died at this early age. So he invited all *The Voice of Healing* ministers to come up on the platform to join hands and pray for the man. I started up there to pray for him.

As I started to walk up the aisle to the platform, the Lord said to me, "Don't go up there." I stopped dead still, and asked, "Why not, Lord? He's only thirty-eight years old. He's not old enough to die." Three years and some months had gone by, and I'd momentarily forgotten what the Lord had told me about him.

The Lord said to me, "He wouldn't judge himself and walk in love toward his fellow ministers, so I judged him and turned him over to Satan for the destruction of his flesh that his spirit may be saved in the day of the Lord Jesus. You leave him alone because he's going to die." So I turned around and walked back up the aisle.

My wife came from another part of the building and met me as I got to the back of the auditorium. She asked, "What did the Lord say to you?"

I said, "How do you know He said anything?"

She said, "Well, you stopped dead still and turned as white as a sheet."

So I told her what the Lord had said. That time, the Lord only mentioned the fact that this evangelist hadn't judged himself on not walking in love toward others. Well, dying prematurely at thirty-eight years old wasn't God's best for him, but it sure beats going to hell!

You see, sometimes there's a reason folks are sick and die prematurely. And before you can get them healed, sometimes you'll have to get down to the root cause why they are sick, and they'll need to make some adjustments.

This minister would put his tent up and hold meetings for a local church in a particular city every year.

The other churches in the city would come and cooperate with him, and thousands of people would come to
the meetings and get saved and healed. They'd fill up
the tent and run it over with people.

But then he announced, "I'm going to build a revival
center in this town," and he built it not very far from
the local church that had helped him hold the meetings.

Then one day he went to the pastor of that local
church, and told him, "I'm going to start my church on
your members and Brother So-and-so's members and
Brother So-and-so's members." And that's exactly what
he did.

Now there was nothing wrong with him starting a
church in that town. But there was something wrong
with him taking two hundred members from one pastor's church, two or three hundred members from
another church, and several hundred members from the
largest Full Gospel church in town! But do you know
what? Before he could enjoy his new church "growth,"
he was dead.

You see, this evangelist worked ill to his fellow pastors. He built his new church, but he built it on the
other fellow's members. Love worketh no ill to his
neighbors.

A person like that is flirting with death! This man
died at an early age because he didn't walk in love
toward his brethren. And that's exactly the reason some
believers die prematurely — they are shortening their
days by not walking in love. We've got to learn to discern the Lord's Body — our brothers and sisters in

Christ — and treat them like they are part of the Lord's Body.

The man wouldn't repent, so God had to judge him. That wasn't God's best, but if a person won't judge himself, he will fall under the penalty of God's judgment. That didn't have to happen to him. But he is the one who was responsible for it happening to him.

It's a solemn thought to fall under the penalty of God's judgment, isn't it? Well, that's why we need to think soberly on the subject of walking in love.

Remember, the Bible says that God's love is greater than faith or hope: *"And now abideth faith, hope, charity, these three; but the greatest of these is charity* [love]*"* (1 Cor. 13:13). We in the Body of Christ haven't majored on the subject of God's love as we should have.

ROMANS 12:9
9 Let love be without dissimulation. Abhor that which is evil; cleave to that which is good.

Sometimes we read this verse, but we don't stop and think about what it means. The word "dissimulation" means *to pretend* or *pretension.* A lot of people pretend they love you, but it doesn't show up in facts. What do I mean by that? They say, "I sure do love you," but you don't dare turn your back on them! They are just pretending that they love you.

ROMANS 12:10
10 Be kindly affectioned one to another with brotherly love; in honour PREFERRING ONE ANOTHER.

Love — God's love — is not selfish. It always prefers the other person and puts him first. It never thinks of itself first. When God told us to love one another, He didn't mean with words only or with pretense. He meant for us to love one another by our actions as well as with our words. Our actions should show that we love one another.

You've got to walk in love toward others, even if they do you wrong. Walking in love toward others pays rich dividends! And if you'll judge yourself, you'll not be judged. If you judge yourself, it will keep you from having medical bills to pay. But you have to purpose in your heart to walk in love. It won't just happen automatically.

When you discern the Lord's body — not only the physical body of Jesus that was broken for your physical healing, but the spiritual Body of Christ — you can be strong and healthy, not weak and sickly. Then you can fulfill the number of your days!

And to tell you the real truth about the matter, God has something more than healing for us. Now, of course, if you need healing, then God has provided healing for you in the Atonement. But God has also provided something more — and that is for us to walk in health. And the way you receive health is to walk in love.

Make the Necessary Adjustments

Sometimes people have come to my meetings who were seeking healing, and sometimes I laid hands on them several times, yet they weren't healed. Other healing evangelists had prayed for them, too, with no results.

But many times when these same people made adjustments in their love walk, they never needed anyone to lay hands on them, they were just automatically healed. You see, walking in love is an area of divine healing that needs to be preached too.

Most of us want to live out our full length of time on this earth. And the Bible promises that we can. But to do so, we will have to walk in the light of the Word, including this Scripture here in First Corinthians 11:31 about judging ourselves.

If someone wants to go to the post office, and I tell him how to get there, it's his fault if he never arrives at his destination. It's the same thing with divine healing and receiving the blessings of God — including long life. The Bible tells us exactly how to arrive at our destination, but we've got to walk in the light of the Word to receive those blessings.

I pastored for nearly twelve years. And in twelve years of pastoring, only two or three of my church members were healed instantly. Before the majority of the people received healing, I had to get down to the cause of why they were sick in the first place.

I don't mean that I accused people who were sick of wrongdoing or sin or started digging in their past. But I'd simply pray that the Holy Ghost would show me if there was anything hindering them. And I would pray that He would show them where they needed to make adjustments.

In every case I dealt with, as soon as the people rectified the cause and made adjustments in their hearts and in their attitudes, they got healed. If they hadn't made the necessary adjustments, some of them would have died because their conditions were that serious.

The Destruction of the Flesh

We can see the consequences of not judging ourselves by this passage in First Corinthians 5.

> **1 CORINTHIANS 5:1-5**
> **1   It is reported commonly that there is fornication among you, and such fornication as is not so much as named among the Gentiles, that one should have his father's wife.**
> **2   And ye are puffed up, and have not rather mourned, that he that hath done this deed might be taken away from among you.**
> **3   For I verily, as absent in body, but present in spirit, have judged already, as though I were present, concerning him that hath so done this deed,**
> **4   In the name of our Lord Jesus Christ, when ye are gathered together, and my spirit, with the power of our Lord Jesus Christ,**
> **5   TO DELIVER SUCH AN ONE UNTO SATAN FOR THE DESTRUCTION OF THE FLESH, that the spirit may be saved in the day of the Lord Jesus.**

In this passage of Scripture, a son had evidently taken his stepmother away from his daddy and was living with her. Paul was surprised at the Church at Corinth because they hadn't done anything about it.

Paul told the Corinthians that when they came together, they were to deliver such a one to Satan for the destruction of his flesh so that his spirit would be saved in the day of Christ.

You see, the church body could judge that sin because it was obvious. In other words, it's easy to judge that it is wrong for a man to live with his step-mother, isn't it? Or if a man is just living with a woman and they're not married, it's easy to judge that that is a sin. And the Church needs to deal with Christians in the church who are doing those things.

We can see in this passage of Scripture in First Corinthians 5 that the Church has a whole lot more authority and power than we've ever exercised. Evidently the Church at Corinth didn't understand or realize that they had authority to do something about that situation.

This Scripture also tells us who it is that destroys the flesh. Verse 5 says, "Turn him over to *Satan* for the destruction of the flesh." Satan destroys the flesh, not God!

Have you ever noticed that sometimes those people who have really known God but then walked away from Him will turn back to Him when their flesh starts getting destroyed?

Evidently this fellow repented and got healed. In Paul's second letter to the Corinthians, Paul told the Corinthians to take this man back into their fellowship because godly sorrow had worked repentance (2 Cor. 2:6-11; 7:10).

What does the Bible say about judging ourselves? It says that if we would judge ourselves, we would not be judged by the Lord. But if we refuse to judge ourselves, then the Lord has to chasten us so we won't be condemned with the world.

That's not God's best, but it sure beats going to hell. You see, in the case of this man who was living with his stepmother, the Bible told the Church to turn him over to Satan for the destruction of his flesh so the man would repent and turn back to God.

Then here in First Corinthians 11:31 and 32, the Bible said that if we won't judge ourselves, the Lord will judge us. Well, the Lord will judge us for more than just physical sins. He will also judge us for spiritual sins.

Only the Lord can see spiritual sins. In fact, Jesus told me once when He appeared to me in a vision, "I'll judge My people more quickly on spiritual sins than I will on physical sins."

What did He mean by "spiritual sins"? Well, for instance, spiritual sins are hidden motives and attitudes. You and I don't know the motives behind people's actions, but Jesus does.

You can't see motives. People can do the right thing for the wrong motive and get a demerit instead of a blessing because their motive is all wrong; it's not based on love.

You and I can't see attitudes, but God can. Our motives and priorities have to be right or God can't bless us like He wants to. That's why it's so important to develop the God-kind of love so our motives are pure.

Now, for instance, with the evangelist in the days of *The Voice of Healing* that I referred to earlier, the Lord waited for this minister to judge himself and put away sin. But the minister never did judge himself and walk in love toward his fellow brethren. So God finally had to judge him.

Then some dear Christians who don't know the Bible say, "That fellow had a great healing ministry, yet he died at thirty-eight. That proves that healing is not for everyone!"

No, that doesn't prove healing is not for everyone! When you know the background, you just simply know that the man wouldn't judge himself, so God had to judge him. God chastened him so he wouldn't be condemned with the world.

Are You Shortening Your Days Or Lengthening Them?

You see, we can shorten our days or we can lengthen them by walking in love and by doing what God has told us to do. We need to judge ourselves so the Lord won't have to judge us. We need to judge ourselves primarily in this area of walking in love and discerning the Body of Christ. Then we won't have to be condemned with the world.

When my wife and I were still living in Texas, I went to pray for a man who had fluid in his lungs and was having difficulty breathing. The doctors had diagnosed him with cancer of the lungs. They said his lungs could only be drained so many times, and then they wouldn't be able to do anything else for him.

I was standing on one side of his bed to pray for this man, and his brother-in-law was standing on the other side. I reached my hand out, laid it on the sick man's forehead, and started praying.

As I prayed, I felt a warm hand take ahold of my hand and take it off his head. I opened my eyes and looked at the man. I thought maybe he had pulled my hand off his head because I was pressing too hard on his forehead.

So I put my hand on the man again, shut my eyes, and started praying. But the same thing happened again. I felt a warm hand take my hand off his forehead. This time I kept my eyes open. I again laid my hand on his forehead with my eyes wide open. I couldn't see anything, but I felt a warm hand just take my hand off his head.

I finally said to the Lord, "Lord, why did You take my hand off him?"

The Lord said, "Because he's going to die."

I said, "But, Lord, he's only forty-three years old. You promised us long life. He's not old enough to die. How come he's going to die?"

The Lord said, "I've been waiting on him for thirty years to judge himself and put away sin and live right. He was saved when he was thirteen years old.

"I healed him one time of a broken back when he left his wife and was living in adultery. I waited on him for thirty years but he wouldn't judge himself, so I judged him and turned him over to Satan for the destruction of his flesh so his spirit may be saved in the day of the Lord Jesus. So you just leave him alone and let him come on home. He's ready now."

Well, that was all revelation to me because *I* didn't know any of that about the man. But I don't just accept something just because it happens. I check up on it. The Bible said, *"Prove all things, hold fast that which is good"* (1 Thess. 5:21).

So I talked to his sister. I told her what the Lord had said to me. She said, "Yes, that's exactly right. He left his wife and was living with another woman. One day he was working on a building, fell off a scaffold, and broke his back."

This man's sister told me that the woman he was living with wouldn't take care of him, so he went back to his wife. He got to praying and got back into fellowship with God. Then he told his wife, "I'm healed!" and wanted the doctor to cut that cast off him.

The doctor told him, "No, I can't do that. If I take that cast off now, you'll turn black and blue all over and fall dead on the floor."

Well, the fellow finally convinced his sister to get the butcher knife and help him cut that cast off. Then he got out of bed, and just like the doctor had said, he turned black and blue and fell on the floor like he was dead. But then suddenly, he rose up completely healed. But he still didn't judge himself.

God had told me, "I healed his back and waited on him for thirty years to judge himself and put away sin."

Well, standing in that bedroom praying for the man, when the Lord told me not to pray for him, I didn't pray for him. The man asked me to take him down to the hospital so they could drain his lungs. After they drained his lungs, he could breathe better, so he came back home. He wasn't bedfast.

That afternoon my wife and I drove to East Texas to hold a meeting. We started the meeting on Sunday. On Sunday night, the phone rang, and it was this man's sister on the phone.

She said, "My brother went home to be with the Lord just a little while ago."

Then she told us what happened. She said, "The doctor came out and had Sunday dinner with us." This man's case was terminal, but he wasn't near death at that time. He could still go to the table and eat Sunday dinner with them.

She related, "My brother asked the doctor, 'Doc, how much more time do I have?'

"'Oh,' the doctor said, 'you don't have to worry about dying for another six months. We can only drain your lungs so many times. But the doctors are constantly working on a cure for cancer, and we might come up with a cure by then.'

"My brother said, 'It may surprise you to know that I'm going home at 10:20 tonight.'"

After dinner his sister went on to church. She told the pastor that her brother had said he was going home to be with the Lord at 10:20 that evening.

Her brother couldn't go to church because he'd get to coughing and just disrupt the service. So he just stayed at home. After the service, the pastor drove by his house to check up on him. It was in the summertime, so the man was sitting out on the porch.

The pastor told his sister, "I drove up to the curb and started talking to him." The house was fairly close to the curb, so the pastor just sat in his car and talked to the fellow.

"I said to him, 'How are you doing?'

"He said, 'Fine.'

"I thought to myself, *It's nearly 10 o'clock right now, and he looks fine to me. He's not going to die at 10:20! Here he is sitting on the front porch talking to me.* So I came on home.

"I had just barely gotten in the front door," this pastor said, "when the telephone rang. It was this man's sister. She told me, 'My brother died at 10:20, just like he said he would.'"

Now that wasn't God's best. It wasn't God's perfect will for him to die at forty-three years of age. It was God's will for him to live out his full length of time down here without sickness or disease, but the man wouldn't judge himself and walk in love.

The Bible said, "For this *cause* many are weak and sickly and die prematurely." You see, there are *causes* why people die prematurely.

It's not God's best that His people don't live out their full length of time down here on this earth. But that's why we need to judge ourselves and make sure we walk in love. If you judge yourself, you'll not be judged by the Lord.

What does it mean to judge yourself? It means that when you see that you've missed it, judge yourself on sin! Just say, "Lord, what I did was wrong. Please forgive me."

I held a meeting for a fellow once who was just a little bit older than I was. I was only about twenty-eight years old at the time, and he was about thirty. He was married, had two children, and was the pastor of a good church that was doing well.

But I could see that something was wrong and that if he kept walking like he was walking, he was going to get into trouble. His wife and his children would come to the table to eat dinner, and they'd be almost shaking, they were so afraid of him.

The fellow would get mad and begin to abuse his wife. Finally she developed stomach problems because she was so nervous. Those little kids would come to the dinner table, and they were so scared of him, they were almost shaking.

The fellow would throw mad fits and go through the house knocking things over. If something didn't suit him just right, he'd knock dishes off the table. This man was a pastor!

I stayed in the parsonage with him and his family, so I tried to talk to him about it. I said to him, "You're going to ruin your wife's health if you keep this up.

You're going to ruin your children's lives, and if you keep on, eventually you'll lose them. If you keep going like this, you're going to cut your own days short."

I said, "Your children have the impression that God is like you are. And they're going to grow up and act like you do."

He never would listen to me, and he wouldn't judge himself and walk in love toward his family.

In the course of time, this pastor's oldest boy grew up and got married. He was saved and filled with the Spirit, but he began acting just like his daddy did. He'd get angry about something, and he'd throw those mad fits. His wife wouldn't put up with it. She left him and went back home to live with her parents.

Well, he got mad about it and decided that he was going to go over to her parents' house and get her. So he went to his daddy-in-law's house. He pounded on the door, and said, "She's my wife, and I've come after her." His daddy-in-law wouldn't open the door. He just talked to him through the door because he knew how he got when he threw those mad fits.

His daddy-in-law said, "She's not going with you! Her health is ruined, and her nerves are shot. She may be your wife all right, but until you learn to act like a man and a gentleman, she's staying right here."

"No! She's my wife, and I'm coming in to get her. I'll knock the door down if I have to!"

He knocked the door down and his daddy-in-law emptied both barrels of a shotgun right into his face, killing him instantly.

Well, I'd told that pastor, this young man's father, that his children were going to wind up that way. Also, in the course of time the pastor's wife's health was ruined. He ended up quitting the ministry when he was just in his mid-50s because he was in such bad health.

Then some people said, "Here this preacher who had that good Full Gospel church is sick and in bad health. That just proves that healing is not for everyone." Yet that had nothing to do with it. If only he had judged himself and walked in love! That was the last church he ever pastored.

This man just wouldn't judge himself and put away sin. He wouldn't walk in love toward his wife and his children. God didn't have anything to do with his bad health or his children turning out that way. The fellow did it to himself because he wouldn't judge himself, change, and treat his family right.

I don't know about you, but I'm going to judge myself. And when I see I've missed it, I'm not even going to wait until I get to church! I'm going to judge myself right then and there and straighten up anything that needs to be straightened up, so I can enjoy God's healing and health and all of His best blessings in life. I want to prolong my days, not cut them short.

When Faith *Won't* Work

If you're not walking in love, your faith won't work. It's that simple. If your faith is failing you, you need to check up on yourself in your love walk.

GALATIANS 5:6
6   . . . faith . . . worketh by love.

I once knew a particular person, who thought everyone was wrong but him. This man criticized any person you would mention. And then he had the audacity to say, "Well, I tried that faith business, and it won't work."

No, his faith wouldn't work because he didn't walk in love. And not only was he not walking in love, but then he insulted God and insulted the Bible by saying, "Faith doesn't work."

Well, if faith doesn't work, then Jesus lied in Mark 11:24 when he said, " . . . *What things soever ye desire, when ye pray, believe that ye receive them, and ye shall have them.*" But, of course, Jesus didn't lie about it.

If there's any failure, it's not on God's part or on Jesus' part. God never fails. And His Word never fails either! So we might just as well admit that if there's any failure, it has to be on our part. What we need to do is check up and find out where we missed it and get ourselves back in line with the Word.

I knew two preachers who had been successful in the ministry for a number of years, and both of them died at an early age. I'll tell you exactly why they died. One of them said to me, "I know you're right, but I'd rather just go ahead and die than to admit I'm wrong."

The other one said basically the same thing. I'd known this Full Gospel Pentecostal evangelist years before. I hadn't seen him for a number of years, but I was holding a meeting in another state, and I ran into this man's brother-in-law.

I asked him, "Whatever happened to Brother C_____?"

"Oh," he said, "he died."

"He died!" I said. "He wasn't old enough to die. He was only in his fifties."

"Yes, but he died."

"Well," I asked, "what was wrong with him?"

His brother-in-law said, "He had cancer. But you know how he was. He would never admit he was wrong about anything. I knew exactly why he didn't get his healing."

You know, sometimes folks won't listen to you because you're their kinfolk. I had even tried to talk to this fellow. When I talked to him, he told me, "No, no, I've never missed it since I've been born again and become a Christian. I've never missed it. I'm perfect!"

Why, a fellow like that is going to die! Nobody's perfect but Jesus. But, you see, he wouldn't judge himself and put away sin and wrongdoing. That doesn't mean he did something flagrantly wrong or something terribly bad. But he just insisted that he'd never missed it in life.

His brother-in-law told me, "I knew he needed to ask some of his kinfolks to forgive him. But he wouldn't admit that he'd ever done anything wrong so he never got it straightened out with them. Everyone else was wrong but him."

Well, now, if a fellow is like that, his faith won't work for him. For one thing, God can't bless him because he's not in the place of God's blessing.

Well, praise God! When I see I'm wrong, I'm going to change, aren't you? I'm not going to be hard-headed about it, and say that I'm right when I'm wrong.

How important it is to walk in love! Do you want God's best in your life? Do you want to live out your full length of time on this earth? You'll never attain God's best in this life unless you purpose in your heart to walk in love. I don't know about you, but I'm targeting for God's best. I'm not satisfied with second best.

How can you make sure you get God's best in life? Judge yourself on sin. That doesn't mean to judge anyone else on sin. The Bible only says to judge *yourself* (Rom 14:13; I Cor. 11:31,32). Judge yourself on your love walk and on how you treat the Body of Christ.

Then put away sin and practice walking in love in every area of your life. Love works no ill to his neighbor, so stop and think every time before you act or say something. Ask yourself, *How is this going to affect the other person?* And *What would love do?*

If what you are about to say or do would work ill to the other person, then don't do it or say it because you wouldn't be walking in love. Every step out of love is sin. But walking in love is fulfilling the Law.

I'm talking about the God-kind of love that is patient and kind. God's love never boils over with jealousy. It is not boastful or vainglorious. It does not display itself haughtily.

God's love in us does not insist on its own rights or on its own way, for it is not self-seeking. It is not touchy or fretful or resentful. It takes no account of the evil done to it. It pays no attention to a suffered wrong.

If you'll learn how to walk in God's love, it will cure any situation that exists. I don't care what the situation is, God's love will cure it if you'll just walk in it.

Of course, the God-kind of love won't work if *you* don't work it. What do I mean by work it? I mean that you have to exercise and develop the God-kind of love that's already in your heart before you will start reaping the rewards that the love of God brings.

For instance, suppose someone went to the doctor, and the doctor gave the person a prescription for what was wrong with him. The person filled the prescription and went home, but he just put the medicine beside the bed and didn't take any of it. Well, the doctor told him the dosage to take, but if the person doesn't take it, it won't work.

The next day, when the person gets worse, he says, "I don't understand it! This medicine isn't working!" But the medicine isn't going to work just sitting on the table.

It's the same way with spiritual things. The Bible is not going to work just laying on the table beside your bed. No, you've got to get it out and put those spiritual truths into operation in your life. Then the blessings of God will manifest in your life.

The love of God is like that too. God's love in you is not going to work just because it's *in* you! You've got to feed on the Word and exercise it by practicing it, and then it will grow and increase.

But if you don't walk in love, eventually you'll be judged by the Lord. And it can cost you your life.

It's just better to walk in love. God's love will work for you! Since sickness is satanic oppression, when you're walking in love and Satan comes along with any of his sickness, you can just say to him, "Satan, I'm walking in love! Take your hands off me."

You can also do that with your little children as long as they are under your jurisdiction. When they grow up, they'll have to do it for themselves.

If you haven't been walking in love, run as fast as you can and get back in the love walk. If you have to repent and ask someone to forgive you, do it.

God's love always prevails! God's love always wins. And love never fails, fades out, or comes to an end. Love always forgives. So forgive so you can live in victory!

The Bible tells us exactly how to receive what has already been provided for us in Christ, but it's up to each of us to follow His instructions so we can arrive at our destination — God's highest and best in our lives. Walking in the love of God is the way to do that.

Chapter 8
Love Your Enemies

Throughout the Gospels, Jesus talked about prayer, and He gave us principles that tell us how we can have an effective prayer life. But it is interesting that the first statement Jesus made in the Gospels relative to prayer was about praying for our enemies.

We'll see that praying for our enemies has a lot to do with walking in the God-kind of love. It also has much to do with whether or not our prayers are heard and answered.

MATTHEW 5:43-48
43 Ye have heard that it hath been said, Thou shalt love thy neighbour, and HATE THINE ENEMY.
44 But I say unto you, LOVE YOUR ENEMIES, BLESS THEM that curse you, DO GOOD to them that hate you, and PRAY FOR THEM which despitefully use you, and persecute you;
45 That ye may be the children of your Father which is in heaven: for he maketh his sun to rise on the evil and on the good, and sendeth rain on the just and on the unjust.
46 For if ye love them which love you, what reward have ye? do not even the publicans the same?
47 And if ye salute your brethren only, what do ye more than others? do not even the publicans so?
48 Be ye therefore perfect [mature], even as your Father which is in heaven is perfect.

Sometimes people wonder what to pray for. Well, think about it for a moment. This is the first recorded statement we have from the lips of Jesus concerning prayer. And the first thing He told us to pray for was our enemies!

It's interesting to note what Jesus said in this passage of Scripture. But to get a better idea of what Jesus was really saying, you have to understand that He was talking to the Jews. You need to know the background of the Jews to understand how powerful this passage of Scripture really is.

If you read the first five Books of the Bible, you would understand that the Jews were well versed in the Law. But did you ever notice that the Old Testament Law didn't teach the Israelites about love, grace, or forgiveness for their enemies?

You won't find principles of loving your enemies taught under the Law — you'll find retribution and judgment. You see, under the Law, the principle was, "An eye for an eye and a tooth for a tooth" (Exod. 21:24). Even when you read the psalms of David, you see him praying against his enemies. He was trying to get the Lord to hate them as he hated them.

That's why in teaching about the God-kind of love, Jesus started out by saying, "You have heard it said that you should love your neighbor and hate your enemy" (v. 43). That's all the Jews had ever heard.

The only Bible the Jews had was the Old Testament. But the Jews didn't even have that in their homes. The Old Testament Law was written on scrolls, and the Law was read in the synagogue on the Sabbath. So all the Jews had ever heard was that they were to love their neighbors and hate their enemies.

But now Jesus said something entirely different. The Jews had never heard about the royal law of love — the God-kind of love. No one had heard of the love of God until Jesus Himself began to teach the people about it. The first time the Jews ever heard about the God-kind of love was right here when Jesus said, *"But I say unto you, Love your enemies . . . ."*

You won't be able to love your enemies unless you are born again and the nature in your heart is changed. It takes divine love to love your enemies. When your spirit is born again, it is recreated in Christ Jesus. Then you can love your enemies.

That's the reason these Jews couldn't understand Jesus — they didn't have a new nature. Also, they'd been taught about a God of judgment. They hadn't heard about a God of love, forgiveness, and compassion. This was all new to them.

Now let's go back and analyze what Jesus was saying in this passage of Scripture in Matthew chapter 5. First, we've got to understand that Jesus was talking about maturing in the God-kind of love. Look at verse 48: *"Be ye therefore perfect, even as your Father which is in heaven is perfect."*

Don't take this verse out of context and make it say something it doesn't say. The word "perfect" here just means *mature.*

Jesus knew none of us could be perfect as God is perfect. But Jesus was saying that we are to grow up and be perfect or *mature* in the God-kind of love.

Notice that Jesus isn't giving us a suggestion in this Scripture. He directed and instructed us to mature in the God-kind of love!

Well, in order to be mature in *God's* love, who are we going to have to love? Just those who love us? No, Jesus said that to be mature in God's love, we'll have to love even our enemies! Our enemies! The Jews had never heard that before.

Then Jesus defined our enemies and told us exactly who they are. He said, " . . . *bless them that curse you, do good to them that hate you, and pray for them which despitefully use you, and persecute you"* (v. 44).

Therefore, our enemies are people who curse us, hate us, use us, and persecute us for the gospel's sake.

Well, according to Jesus, what are we to do to our enemies? Are we to retaliate and get even with them? No, we are to *love* them, *bless* them, do *good* to them, and *pray* for them.

The thought here is that if we will do these things for those who hate us, we will mature in the God-kind of love. Then we will be acting like our Heavenly Father.

Show God's Love to Your Enemies

You remember that First John 4:8 says that God is love. The Bible also says that God is perfect or mature in love. Well, God loves His enemies, so if we're going to be like Him, we have to love our enemies.

Does God love His enemies? Yes, He does. For example, we read in the New Testament that God loved us while we were yet sinners or enemies of the Cross of Calvary.

ROMANS 5:8-10
8   But God commendeth his love toward us, in that, while we were yet sinners, Christ died for us.
9   Much more then, being now justified by his blood, we shall be saved from wrath through him.
10 For if, when we were enemies, we were reconciled to God by the death of his Son, much more, being reconciled, we shall be saved by his life.

Now God is telling us to do the same thing He did. We are to love our enemies just as He loved His enemies.

Well, how can we love our enemies? One way God tells us to love our enemies is to bless them when they curse us. Did God do that? Yes, He did.

While we were yet sinners, God poured out His blessings upon us by giving us the Gift of His Son, Jesus Christ, as our Savior. God forgave us in Jesus, even before we were saved. Of course, we had to *accept* God's salvation, but God's free gift of eternal life was already provided for us while we were yet sinners.

Not only that, but then the Bible says that God blessed us with all spiritual blessings in Christ (Eph. 1:3). Those blessings belong to everyone who receives Jesus, whether folks accept those blessings or not.

In other words, God so loved the world that He showed His love by giving us all spiritual blessings in Jesus, even when we were yet sinners and didn't accept God's love to mankind.

And even now all of God's heavenly blessings in Christ belong to even the worst sinner who is an enemy to the Cross of Calvary, if he will just repent and accept Jesus Christ as his Savior.

But all of God's blessings won't do a person any good unless he accepts Jesus Christ as his Savior and receives all of God's free blessings.

Then Jesus said something else about the God-kind of love. He said, *"For if ye love them which love you, what reward have ye? do not even the publicans the same?"* (Matt. 5:46).

Jesus said that if we only love those who love us, what reward do we have in Heaven? Even the publicans love those who love them. If we're good only to our brethren and our friends, we are not doing any more than unsaved people do.

It's easy to love your friends, isn't it? They are lovely, and they treat you right. But enemies are not lovely. They don't act lovely, and they don't treat you right.

But isn't it interesting that those are the exact people that Jesus said we Christians are to love! Then notice something else Jesus said in this verse. He said,

"What reward do you have if you only love those who love you?"

You see, there is a reward in Heaven for loving our enemies. How many of us want to receive God's reward for loving those who hate us? I don't know about you, but I do!

And often unless we obey this verse, our prayers won't be answered because we're not being doers of the Word. After all, if we abide in Him, and God's Word abides in us, then we are going to be doers of this Scripture too.

How *can* you love your enemies? You won't be able to do that unless you've been born again, and the love of God is in you. The natural man can't do that in the energy of the flesh. It's impossible. But the love of God in our hearts makes it possible.

Do Good to Your Enemies

Then Jesus tells us to do good to those who hate us. Does God do good to those who hate him? Yes, He does. Matthew 5:45 says, " . . . *he* [God] *maketh his sun to rise on the evil and on the good, and sendeth rain on the just and on the unjust.*"

Remember, Jesus told us that we are to act just like our Heavenly Father: *"That ye may be the children of your Father which is in heaven . . . "* (v. 45). That's a strong statement.

If you take the negative side of that statement, you could say it this way: "If you aren't good to your enemies, then you aren't acting like the children of your Heavenly Father." Actually, you're not walking in the light as He is in the light (1 John 1:7).

So Jesus is saying to us, "Act just like your Heavenly Father. He loves His enemies and does good to them, so you do the same." And God's Word teaches us that we are to overcome evil with good (Rom. 12:21).

If you know someone who hates you, find something good that you can do for him. Buy him a gift, or send him a special love offering. Pray for him. It's amazing how people respond to love.

You see, this is how we will act if we are mature in the God-kind of love. We will act like our Heavenly Father and love people whether or not we think they deserve it.

I remember hearing of a woman minister who once told about an incident that happened to her along this line. She began holding meetings in a certain city, and another minister in that town didn't believe in women ministers. He happened to have a radio program, and on his program he called her by name and said things about her that weren't right. He persecuted her publicly.

So this woman minister said to the Lord, "Lord, I'm not going to let that bother me. What can I do to help this man?" She realized that he was struggling in his ministry, trying to pay for his church, so she just took up an offering and sent it to him. Well, it wasn't long before he invited her to speak in his church!

Do good to those who hate you. That's God's way. Repay evil with good. Find out something you can do for those who have mistreated you. Ask the Lord how you can be a blessing to those who have wronged you. Returning kindness for evil works because that's what Jesus taught us to do.

I remember one particular minister years ago who didn't agree with the things I was preaching, so he criticized me. Some time later he happened to get into trouble in his ministry. I called him personally and said, "I just wanted to call and let you know that I'm for you. I believe in you. I just wanted you to know that I'm praying for you."

You see, we shouldn't be throwing stones at people; we should be finding ways to do them good! We should find ways to help people if we can. This minister told me how much my encouragement helped him.

Then he told someone else, "One thing about it! When something happens and you get down, you really find out who your friends are." Then he said to someone else, "I found out among other things that I was just wrong about Brother Hagin."

Pray for Your Enemies

In this particular passage of Scripture, when Jesus talks about our being perfect or mature in the God-kind of love, He's talking about our being mature in love *and* in prayer. If we have a mature prayer life, we will pray for our enemies, not criticize them or talk about them.

We are to pray for those who despitefully use us and persecute us. Was Jesus persecuted in His earthly ministry? Of course He was. Jesus' enemies crucified Him.

You might say, "But you just don't understand what people have done to me."

Well, Jesus is our Example, and look what people did to Him! He is the One who said we are to pray for our enemies. Did He pray for His enemies? If He did, then we should follow His example.

Notice what Jesus did when He was hanging on the Cross, bleeding, hurting, and dying. Did He rail against His enemies and accuse them? No, He prayed for them. In fact, He prayed for the very people who were crucifying Him. He prayed, " . . . *Father, forgive them; for they know not what they do"* (Luke 23:34).

Some say, "Yes, but that was Jesus. *He* could do that because He's the Son of God."

But the same love that was in Jesus' heart has been shed abroad in our hearts by the Holy Spirit. Jesus wouldn't ask us to do something that was impossible for us to do.

As a young Baptist boy preacher before I even had the baptism in the Holy Spirit, I read this statement from the Master's lips: "Pray for those who despitefully use you and persecute you." So I began to practice this principle way back then. When anyone mistreated me, I just prayed for him.

I'd pray, "God, bless dear Brother So-and-so. I may not understand why he said what he said, but that's between him and You. But I know You want to bless him, so I pray that you will bless his ministry and give him divine guidance and direction in every area of his life. Lord, use him, and make him a blessing to others."

I want good things to happen to people, not bad things. I don't want to see anyone miss it, do you? So even when people criticize me, I don't pray that something bad will happen to them! I pray that they'll be blessed.

And we do have examples of those in the New Testament who forgave their enemies, prayed for them, and let the love of God dominate them.

The Love of God in Action

Stephen was an example of a person who acted in love toward his enemies. He let the love of God dominate him.

Stephen was the first martyr for the gospel of the Lord Jesus Christ that we have recorded in the Bible. The persecutors of the Early Church stoned him to death, and as he lay dying, Stephen prayed for those who were killing him.

ACTS 7:59,60
59 And they stoned Stephen, calling upon God, and saying, Lord Jesus, receive my spirit.
60 And he kneeled down, and cried with a loud voice, LORD, LAY NOT THIS SIN TO THEIR CHARGE. And when he had said this, he fell asleep.

Praying for those who are stoning you certainly demonstrates the love of God in action, doesn't it? When Stephen's enemies were stoning him, he prayed for them and asked God not to lay that sin to their charge.

If you're going to let the flesh dominate you, you'll want to fight back against those who persecute you. You'll want to retaliate and answer them back. But I learned a long time ago that the best thing in the world to do is to just start praying for them.

When people demonstrate the God-kind of love and the kind of self-sacrificing attitude that prays for others, they are going to become people of real prayer.

Those are the people whose voices will be heard on High. They'll get their prayers answered! Why? Because they are *doers* of the Word. And the Bible says that it's the doers of the Word who will be blessed in their deeds (James 1:25).

But if believers aren't going to be doers of the Word, they will just deceive themselves because an effective prayer life has to be based on the Word.

You see, sometimes people wonder why their prayers aren't answered. They don't stop to think that there are hindrances to prayer. Failing to be a doer of the Word by praying for your enemies is one area where prayers can be hindered.

If you don't forgive your enemies and pray for them, it can hinder your own prayer life. But why does God want us to *pray* for them?

For one thing, *you* will know that you have forgiven your enemies when you can pray for them and ask

God's blessings upon them. Praying for those who have wronged you causes you to release the hurts, grudges, and the unforgiveness you have in your heart against them.

I believe that this is the reason Jesus talked about praying for our enemies before He talked about any other kind of prayer. You see, in order to pray for your enemies, you have to get your heart right with God!

In other words, you can't pray for your enemies without forgiving them. And once you can pray God's blessing on them, your heart will no longer condemn you; therefore, you can have confidence before God (1 John 3:20,21).

If believers only realized that they need to have things in the proper perspective in order to get their prayers answered!

Besides that, praying for your enemies blesses *you*. It helps you as much or more than it does them. You will personally feel so much better when you pray for those who have done you wrong.

So if you think someone doesn't like you, pray for him! Find some way to be a blessing to the person. Ask God to show you what you can do to help him or her.

Peter also had something to say in relation to how we are to react to people when they aren't treating us like we think they should.

1 PETER 3:9
9 Not rendering evil for evil, or railing for railing: BUT CONTRARIWISE BLESSING; knowing

that ye are thereunto called, THAT YE SHOULD INHERIT A BLESSING.

There is a blessing when you pray for your enemies instead of rendering evil for evil. The Bible says we are not called to return evil for evil and railing for railing.

That means when someone says something evil to you or about you, you are not to retaliate by saying something evil back. Instead, you are to bless them and do good to them.

Look at this verse in *The Amplified Bible.*

1 PETER 3:9 *(Amplified)*
9   Never return evil for evil or insult for insult — scolding, tongue-lashing, berating; but on the contrary blessing — PRAYING FOR THEIR WELFARE, HAPPINESS AND PROTECTION, AND TRULY PITYING AND LOVING THEM. For know that to this you have been called, THAT YOU MAY YOURSELVES INHERIT A BLESSING [from God] — obtain a blessing as heirs, bringing welfare and happiness and protection.

This verse says that we are to pray for our enemies' welfare, happiness, and protection. And we are to truly pity and love those who hate us.

How many of us can honestly say that we pity and love those who have wronged us? Do we demonstrate our love by praying for their welfare, happiness, and protection? That is the God-kind of love in action.

I want you to see something else about this verse. This verse promises that we will inherit a blessing from God if we will pray for those who do us wrong instead of returning evil for evil and insult for insult. This verse is telling us to act in the God-kind of love so that we can inherit a blessing from God.

Remember Jesus said in Matthew 5:46 that there is a reward in Heaven for loving our enemies. Then in this verse in First Peter, God tells us that we inherit a blessing when we pray for our enemies. God wants us to love our enemies and pray for them because He knows that's when *we* will receive the blessings of God in *our* lives!

In a previous chapter, we looked at First Peter 3:11 and 12 about living a long, good life on the earth. But look at this verse now pertaining to prayer. Peter is also talking about prayer here because he said that the Lord's ears are open to the prayers of the righteous.

1 PETER 3:11,12
11 Let him ESCHEW [avoid or shun] EVIL, and DO GOOD; let him SEEK PEACE, and ENSUE [pursue] it.
12 For the eyes of the Lord are over the righteous, and HIS EARS ARE OPEN UNTO THEIR PRAYERS: but the face of the Lord is against them that do evil.

This verse says basically the same thing Jesus was saying. We are to eschew or avoid evil, do good, and not only seek peace, but pursue peace with everyone, including our enemies.

People can criticize you and talk about you, but that doesn't mean you have a right to criticize or talk about them! No, if you want the Lord's ears to be open to your prayers and if you want His blessings in your life, you are going to have to avoid evil, do good, and seek peace with your enemies, whether they do good to you or not.

And, really, it just feels so much better to walk in the light with God and to pray for those who despitefully use you and persecute you.

Well, if we can't return evil for evil and rail against our enemies, then scripturally what *can* we do so we can receive a reward in Heaven and inherit God's blessing?

Jesus gave us four actions we must take if we are going to mature in prayer and mature in the God-kind of love. These four actions bring God's blessing and reward every single time in our lives. They tell us how we are to treat our enemies. We are to *love* them, *bless* them, do *good* to them, and *pray* for them.

Remember, this is *Jesus* talking! He's telling us exactly how we are to treat our enemies so we can mature and be perfected in the God-kind of love. If we will do these things, the love of God will be perfected in our lives. We will reflect the same kind of love that God is, for God *is* love.

Return Good for Evil and Inherit a Blessing!

One church I pastored had a lot of problems, but somehow or other, God gave me the wisdom to pastor that church, and He solved the problems. When I left that church, the congregation had grown and the church was full and running over. But the fellow who took over the pastorate after me ran into some problems pastoring that church.

I was out in the field ministry by then and just happened to be in that area, so I thought I would drop in and visit with this new pastor. I'd heard he was having some troubles in the church, so I'd been praying for him. In fact, many times God would wake me up early in the morning, and I'd pray for him. I had compassion for him. After all, I'd pastored that church, and I knew some of the problems that existed.

So when I came into town that particular day, I drove up to the parsonage, and this pastor came out to the car to talk to me. I told him I had some business in town and just wanted to stop by to see how he was doing.

I asked him, "How are things going?"

He said, "Things aren't right! People aren't paying their tithes."

Then he looked at me and demanded, "Have you been coming around here collecting these people's tithes?"

When he asked me that, before I could say a word, he got so mad, he just reached in and grabbed ahold of my necktie. I thought he was going to pull me out of the car!

Well, I have the flesh to deal with just like you do. I wanted to knock him in the head, but I knew I couldn't let the flesh dominate me. I could just see the headlines in the local paper, "Full Gospel Minister Knocks Full Gospel Pastor in the Head." But here he was accusing me of stealing the people's tithes!

The Bible said not to render evil for evil or railing for railing. The world's way is that when people rail against you, you just retaliate and rail back against them. But the Bible says, "Contrariwise, render *blessing*, so that you can inherit a blessing."

I said to him, "I haven't received a dime from the people in your church! Dear Brother, I've prayed for you more than once. Why, just the day before yesterday at four o'clock in the morning, I was down on my knees on the cold linoleum floor praying for you!"

You see, I knew problems existed in that church because I had pastored it. God had told me how to deal with the people in that congregation, but now some of those same problems had surfaced again, and this pastor didn't know how to handle them.

When I told this pastor I'd been praying for him, he jumped just like I'd hit him with a whip. Then he started crying, "My God! Brother Hagin, forgive me! I knew what I said wasn't right. I just had to lay off the blame on someone."

Then he admitted, "I've just been such a failure in this church. I haven't handled the situation right, and I've divided the church and run half the people off. You were a success and I wasn't, and I was trying to blame all the trouble off on you. Will you forgive me?"

I said, "Sure, I forgive you." And then we hugged one another and fellowshipped awhile. We parted friends instead of enemies. Isn't that better than fighting?

However, if I had let my flesh rule me, and I'd returned evil for evil and railing for railing, it wouldn't have turned out that way. But because I didn't allow my flesh to take over, that man is my friend to this day.

Practice Staying in an Attitude of Love

On the Cross, Jesus demonstrated the same kind of love He preached about. He not only forgave those who crucified Him, but then He said something interesting. He said, " . . . *Father, forgive them; FOR THEY KNOW NOT WHAT THEY DO . . .* " (Luke 23:34).

Why did Jesus say that? Because so many times people don't realize what they are doing when they fail to walk in love toward others. Many times they don't realize how destructive criticism and persecution are to others. They don't want to sin and miss it, but they just don't understand how harmful criticism is to the other fellow.

Well, if people criticize me, I'm not going to get all flustered and upset about it and miss God's blessings in my life. I'm going to stay in an attitude of love and do what the Bible says in these verses so I don't miss God's best blessings in life.

Actually, in my years of ministry, I've never had any problems with fellow ministers. I just love them; I don't talk about them, and I don't judge them. I'm not going to peddle gossip and talk about other folks. And I'm not going to go around peddling things about other people that will ruin their ministries.

No! I just refuse to do that. I refuse to tell tales about other people. I don't have a slop bucket for an ear, so I'm not going to let someone pour a bunch of slop and gossip in my ear about anyone! It will affect my spiritual progress and my health, and I'm just not going to do it.

Someone asked, "Well, what if it's true?" I'm still not going to do it. Even if someone has missed it, which one of us hasn't missed it some time or another in life? Do you know anyone who hasn't missed it? No, you don't. And neither do I because Jesus was the only perfect Person who has ever walked on this earth.

Since we've all missed it in one way or another, then we just need to keep on loving one another. By keeping the right attitude, whether our flesh feels like it or not, and by just keeping on loving folks, we will reap rich rewards.

The best way to walk in the goodness of the Lord is to walk in love. Practice and exercise the God-kind of love that is already in your heart. Yes, your flesh will want to dominate you, but you don't have to let it. As you practice the God-kind of love, God's love will grow and develop, and you'll be a blessing to many.

But if you are going to harbor resentment and ill will toward other people in your soul and refuse to pray for people when they wrong you, it will affect you not only physically, but spiritually.

You can't afford to meditate on what people have said about you or what they've done to you or how they've persecuted or used you. If you entertain those things in your thought life, those negative thoughts will just fester in your spirit and your soul and eventually begin to affect you in every area of life.

For example, have you ever heard people say, "So-and-so just doesn't like me."

You ask them, "Well, what are you doing about it?"

"I'm never going to speak to him again!"

Then people wonder why their prayers are hindered and their faith won't work!

When I pastored a particular church one time, one night after our Sunday night service, a woman came up to the front of the church to talk to me. People were standing around visiting. We didn't have a foyer; it was just a one-room church that seated about three hundred people.

Anyway, this woman came to me just crying. She said, "I wish you'd pray for me."

"What for, Sister? What's wrong?"

"Well," she said, "Sister So-and-so and Sister So-and-so are standing in the back of the church talking about me."

"Sister," I said smiling, "I'm sure they've got a better subject than that to talk about! Besides, how do you know they're talking about you?"

"Well," she answered, "I just know it."

"Why," I said, "they're no more talking about you than anything in the world. There's no use praying about that. You just need to practice the Word. Besides that, even if they were talking about you, you're supposed to go ahead and love them anyway."

She insisted, "Well, I just know they're talking about me!"

"There's a good way to find out," I said. "Let's go back there and see what they're talking about." So we just walked back to where these ladies were talking inside the church.

I said to them, "What are you ladies talking about?"

Come to find out, they were talking about canning fruit and making preserves. They hadn't been talking about this woman!

Do you see how people are hindered because God's Word isn't abiding in them. Then when they don't walk in the light of the Word, it hinders their prayer life.

You see, this woman just kept meditating on the thought that these other ladies were talking about her until it festered in her soul, and she got so worked up that she needed prayer. She missed a blessing by not practicing the God-kind of love.

Even if these ladies had been talking about this woman, what should she have done about it? She should have loved them anyway, forgiven them, and prayed for them.

Besides, when you are mature in the God-kind of love, you don't let things like that affect you. You just keep on loving people in spite of how they may treat you.

I've learned not to let people's criticism affect me the least bit in the world. I've told people for a good many years that I wouldn't even take time to deny it if someone accused me of killing my grandma. I'd just keep shouting the victory and praising God.

Let people say what they want to about me! I'll pray for them, but I'm not going to let it affect me. As for me, I'm going to keep on worshipping God and staying healthy!

God's Love — The Great Healing Agent

Who are we supposed to pray for? Only those brethren who treat us right? Pray only for those who are good to us? After all, they ought to be blessed since they've been such a blessing to us!

No, you're not just to pray for them! You're to pray for those who despitefully use you and persecute you. If you'll pray for your enemies, it will help you spiritually in other areas too.

Why will you be blessed spiritually in other areas? Because according to James 1:25, it is the doer of the Word who is blessed in his deed. And it's the prayer life based on God's Word that is successful! It's when we pray in line with God's Word that we get results.

Let's just practice what the Bible says! Let's be doers of the Word and not just hearers only. Then things will work out for us in every area of life!

I know from experience and from the Word that if you're going to walk in health, you're going to have to walk close to God. Therefore, you'll have to walk in the God-kind of love because God *is* love. Opportunities will come up all the time in life for you to practice what these verses say about loving your enemies.

You need to understand that you can't violate this Scripture about praying for your enemies, then run around trying to get people to pray for you and get results. Someone else's faith is not going to work for you as long as you are harboring things in your heart against someone else.

It doesn't matter how badly people have treated you or what they've said about you — this verse says to pray for them! You will have to release those hurts and resentments to God and pray for those who have hurt you before you can reap God's best in this life.

I am convinced that if the Body of Christ ever starts really walking in the God-kind of love, there won't be any sickness among us.

Even many in the secular community understand what hate and resentment can do to a person's health. For example, several years ago, I read an account from a doctor who was the head of a large medical association. He made an astonishing statement.

He said, "Actually, love is the greatest healing agency there is."

Then he said something else that was interesting. He said, "The old-fashioned doctor did more than just simply treat people. In those days, doctors used to make home visits. By making home visits, they could see the atmosphere the people lived in day after day." Many times the doctor could see why the people got sick in the first place!

When people live in an atmosphere where there is no love and compassion, it's easy to see how people can get sick. And this doctor was just talking about *human* love.

If walking in natural human love is a great healing agency, just think what a great healing agency walking in *God's* love would be!

In order to stay free from sickness, you're going to have to practice loving your enemies! I've had many opportunities over the years to practice this principle.

For example, an evangelist once held a meeting for me. He did something to me that was wrong and unethical. The devil suggested the thought to me, *If I were you, I wouldn't take up another offering for him.*

That's the get-even nature of the flesh. The flesh always wants to get revenge. But in the Bible, God said, "Revenge is Mine, I will repay" (Heb. 10:30). I have found that it's just better to let the Lord fight your battles. He'll do a better job than you could. If you try to take revenge, you'll get things in a mess.

You see, if you let your natural human reasoning and your flesh dominate you, you'll wind up in trouble because then you're going to want to retaliate. And if you're not careful, your flesh and your mind will side in with the devil, and you'll want to accommodate *his* thoughts.

Anyway, I recognized that the thought to get even with this evangelist came into my mind from the devil. It didn't come from my recreated spirit where the Holy Spirit dwells.

So I said, "Just for that, Mr. Devil, I'm going to take up an offering for that evangelist every night. And if you say anything more about it, I'll take up two offerings for him every night."

Why did I say that? Because the law of love, the God-kind of love, says, "Return good for evil" (Rom. 12:21). And in this verse in Matthew 5:44 it said, *". . . Love your enemies . . . do good to them that hate you . . . ."*

Do you know the devil never said another word to me about that evangelist. The devil doesn't want any preacher getting *two* offerings a night!

So I took up an offering for that evangelist every night. Then I asked the evangelist, "How much do you usually average?" He told me, and I paid him three times as much as he usually got even in the larger churches, and I gave a third of it out of my own pocket.

I did that because I wanted to exercise and develop the God-kind of love. The evangelist went away feeling good. I'd rather it be that way, wouldn't you?

Do good to those who use you and persecute you! The Bible teaches you to do good to all men, not just believers. By doing good to all people, you are fulfilling the royal law of love (James 2:8).

Being a Doer of the Word

In order to be a doer of the Word, you're going to have to love your enemies. That means you'll have to act in love toward your enemies whether you feel like it or not.

JAMES 1:22-25
22 But BE YE DOERS OF THE WORD, and not hearers only, deceiving your own selves.
23 For IF ANY BE A HEARER OF THE WORD, and NOT A DOER, he is like unto a man beholding his natural face in a glass:
24 For he beholdeth himself, and goeth his way, and straightway forgetteth WHAT MANNER OF MAN HE WAS.
25 But whoso looketh into the perfect law of liberty, and continueth therein, he being not a forgetful hearer, but a doer of the work, THIS MAN SHALL BE BLESSED IN HIS DEED.

You see, you can look into the perfect law of liberty — the Word of God — but then go away and forget what manner of man or woman you are. Well, what kind of a person are you?

If you're born again, you are a new creation who is to walk in God's love. That includes being kind, tenderhearted, and not rendering railing for railing or evil for evil, but walking in the fruit of the spirit.

However, if you look into the Word to see the characteristics of the God-kind of love, but then forget what manner of person you're supposed to be, you are only a *hearer* of the Word, not a doer.

A hearer, but not a doer of the Word, walks in the flesh and retaliates instead of walking in love. A doer of the Word walks in the fruit of the spirit. To be a doer of the Word, you will have to continually remember that you are a lover and a forgiver, not a hater.

Jesus told us to pray for our enemies because He knew what would make our voices heard on High. When we love our enemies by praying for them, we are acting like our Heavenly Father. Then we will inherit God's blessing and receive His reward in Heaven. And loving our enemies will cause us to mature in the God-kind of love which never fails.

This is the key and the secret to receiving God's best blessings in life — *love your enemies*. I know from experience that if you are going to walk in health, healing, and all of God's spiritual blessings, you're going to have to love your enemies, do good to them, bless them, and pray for them.

Don't forget what manner of person you are — that you are a born-again new creation in Christ. If someone says to you, "I don't like you," don't forget that you are a lover, not a hater, because the love of God has been shed abroad in your heart. Don't get in the flesh and retaliate.

Instead, just say, "Well, I love you, praise the Lord! And if I can do anything to help you, just let me know. In fact, if there's any way at all that I can be a blessing to you, just let me know, and I will do it." People respond to a humble attitude of love.

The cure for all physical, mental, and spiritual ills is just for Christians to become doers of the Word. So let's preach the cure for hate, which is forgiveness and love. Let's preach the cure for unforgiveness, railing, and strife — the love of God in demonstration.

Do Unto Others . . .

Jesus said something else about loving our enemies. He used different words, but really He was talking about the same subject.

MATTHEW 7:12
12 Therefore ALL THINGS WHATSOEVER YE WOULD THAT MEN SHOULD DO TO YOU, do ye even so to them: FOR THIS IS THE LAW and the prophets.

In other words, Jesus was saying that you don't have to worry about trying to fulfill the Law with all its commandments if you'll just do what the Word says. You will be fulfilling the law of love when you treat others the way you want to be treated.

Do you want everyone to love you? Of course you do. Then you should love everyone. That includes your enemies. If you want your enemies to love you, then you love them first, regardless of how they treat you.

Whatever you want people to do for you, then you do that for them. Wouldn't you want people to bless you instead of curse you? Then you bless them, even if they curse you.

Would you want people to do good to you instead of doing evil to you? Then if they do evil to you, you do good to them.

Wouldn't you want people to pray for you, even if you missed it and said something you shouldn't have said about them? Then you pray for people — even if they are your enemies or if they have said something bad about you.

You see, this is how the God-kind of love — the royal law of love — works. Really, the royal law of love and the golden rule are the same: "Do unto others as you would have them do unto you." That's saying the same thing as "Love your neighbor as yourself." We hear a lot of talk about the golden rule, but we see very little action!

And, actually, the way of the flesh is to "Do unto others *before* they do unto you." It seems like a lot of Christians practice that! They're out to do the other fellow in. Christians who do that are not acting like the children of their Heavenly Father.

Many years ago a fellow who was a lot like that helped me in one of my meetings. But he didn't last long in my ministry when I saw what his motives were. It seemed like he'd practically just lie awake at night trying to figure out how to get money out of people.

We were using the church auditorium of a large Full Gospel church to hold a meeting. Our budget for the meetings included the expenses of a daily radio program, newspaper advertisements, and then our own expenses.

Well, this fellow would make the announcements, and I'd stay back in the speaker room and pray until it was time for me to preach. This fellow and I had made the agreement that once our expenses were met, we would divide whatever money was left over between us, and that would be our support.

We ran the meetings four weeks. After the second week of meetings, this fellow came to me and said, "We've already got enough money to pay for our expenses.

"But let's not tell the people that because they are giving so good. Let's just keep on like we're raising money for the radio program and for the expenses of the meeting."

"No," I said, "that would be lying. We're not going to do that."

"But we're going to miss an opportunity if we don't," he said. "We could really clean up here."

I said, "No, we're not going to do that because we've got our word out. We told the people what we would do, and we're going to do what we said we'd do."

"Well," he said, "I'm the one out there taking up the offering. I'm just going to go ahead and do it."

"No, you're not," I said, "because there's a speaker back there in the room where I'm praying. And if you say that, I'm going to come right out, get on the platform, and tell the folks you're lying."

"Well," he said, "you're going to miss it! I'll tell you that right now! I see that you just don't know how to make it." Well, that was the last time he ever took up an offering for me.

Somehow, no one has heard from that fellow for years, but I'm still out there preaching the Word! Somehow, I managed to make it by telling the truth and by doing unto others as I'd have them do unto me.

Some folks are just out to do in the other fellow. Instead of doing the other fellow in, they should be trying to outdo the other fellow in love!

We ought to try to figure out how to be a blessing to people! We need to be asking ourselves, *How can I bless people? How can I do good to them?*

Did you ever stop to think about it? If you'd just analyze Matthew 7:12, you would find out what Jesus was really saying in this verse.

MATTHEW 7:12
12 . . . all things whatsoever ye would that men should do to you, do ye even so to them. . . .

Jesus was really saying, "If you want good to come to you, *you* do good to *others*."

That is thoroughly scriptural because the Bible says, *"Be not deceived; God is not mocked: for whatsoever a man soweth, that shall he also reap"* (Gal. 6:7). You see, it all comes right back to the same principle — walk in God's love to receive God's best in life.

Every one of us wants to receive all that God has for us in this life. But do you understand that you will never achieve God's best in your life unless you walk in the love of God?

Let God change your life with His love, so that you can be a blessing to others wherever you go. If you want *God* to do good to you, *you* do good to *others*. Walking in God's love is the way to victory in life!

God has a *specific* plan for your life.
Are you ready?
RHEMA Bible Training Center

Mt Ophel - Shiloah   Perry Stone
eyes open

Mirah =

Zion - 2 Chr 5:14
sanctifies

Mirah = H Sp offered

Mh 3:26

Temple Mt platform =
Mt Moriah Gen 14:18-20
22:% Isaac

Heb 5:6,10
Rev 19:16 Kg K & Lord of
Gen 14:18 Jerusalem
Gen 22:14 Jerusalem
2 Chron 3:1

Temple 70 A.D. destroyed
Chambers under ntw. 500 cu sq area.
uncut stones = cut in a Quary
2 chron = Iron - rip firewar & struggle
done out Temple
Joshua 24:27 rocks have heard.
Stones holds sounds in them.
Gen 4:8,10 Blood final sacrifice
Glory of Lord came down.
Christ.
1. white stone & lime stone = is wh in Jerusalem
Leen Ritmeyer
under . ntw levels of Chambers, Dome shape
Jen 15:2:17-22   ark of cov.
Ezra 1:1   Chamber of wood ark is hidden.
Isa. 1998. tel us ark of cov. ark sealed up.
wentin: saw ark of cov. Warren gate
only Priestly can handle it

...derground dig for gold, / underground chambers
...mon Tomb has never been found.
· Rabbi met & Pope to give back Treasures of Israel

ape of Moth =
Shi'yn ↓↑↓ God name
     Dehenm   every Mezoza 🕎 Deut 13:10-11
     fire
ape of N.M. Valley
ah Moriah.. Heb letter, Name of God there
Deut 12:11 Sacred Furniture

Laver veil· www.everything Jewish
   7 candle
   Bread
   ark of cov.
EXODUS
   Altar of Brass Ex 27:1 (Humanity) corner
   Wine + Blood. Ex 27:3+4 grate. ramp to altar x 4
3 grate fires. wood, fire + fire, a back up fire.
   I Thes 5:23
   Matt 27:38
   Heb 10:10
   *Ex. 24:6 poured out w. S.E.W.
   Rom 12:1 offering to God.
   Laver I Corinthian
IK. 7:29-32 16,000 gal water TWIN POOLS
water= sanctified by washing of water of word
   John 19:34
   Matt 3:13-16 sanctification / water Baptism
      out court MINISTRY
Women = Holy place
   3 pieces of furniture = Table of Shewbread

Lev. 8

Lev 24:7g Temple shewbread
made of accia wood, 12 pieces of Bread

Matt 10:10
12 doz
1. sal
fur
reg
sret
10 gold gr
Etern L
12. Eternal punishment
I Chron 5:— 120 sep. pieces of Bread
acts 2:1-4-15 /20
12 disp upper room — 120

EX 25:31 Minorah 7 Br. Gold
Bread renewed   Oil = every day —
        37
James 5:14
solomon added 10 sm Menorah 70 lam

EX 1:5
Num 24:1
Luke 10:17 (70 sent faith Law matter + La
           Elders
7 Branche servant Branch   Rev 1:1-12

Rev 5:6 - (4:5)
    Isa 11:2 (7 sp of God, 1 piece of gold znety
Eph 1:18 Minorah eyes
    7 lamps Isa 11:1-4
3 = 3×3 –9 = 27 N.T.
12 cm — 27 –12 = OT. 66 =

Ps 109: 105, 11

EX 28: 29/30 enquire of LORD